Poems
of
Rabindranath Tagore

Poems
of
Rabindranath Tagore

Poems
of
Rabindranath Tagore

Edited by Humayun Kabir

UBSPD

Project Editor : Moitreyee Chatterjee
Cover Design : Soumik Saha

UBS Publishers' Distributors Pvt. Ltd.
5 Ansari Road, New Delhi-110 002
Phones: 011-23273601-04, 23266646 ● Fax: 23276593, 23274261
E-mail: ubspd@ubspd.com
10 First Main Road, Gandhi Nagar, Bangalore-560 009
Phones: 080-22253903, 22263901, 22263902 ● Fax: 22263904
E-mail: ubspdbng@eth.net
8/1-B Chowringhee Lane, Kolkata-700 016
Phones: 033-22521821, 22522910, 22529473 ● Fax: 22523027
E-mail: ubspdcal@cal.vsnl.net.in
60 Nelson Manickam Road, Aminjikarai, Chennai-600 029
Phones: 044-23746222, 23746351-2 ● Fax: 23746287
E-mail: ubspd@che.ubspd.com
Ground Floor, Western Side, Annaporna Complex,
202 Naya Tola, Patna-800 004
Phones: 0612-2672856, 2673973, 2686170 ● Fax: 2686169
E-mail: ubspdpat1@sancharnet.in
143, M P Nagar, Zone I, Bhopal-462 011
Phones: 0755-5203183, 5203193, 2555228 ● Fax: 2555285
E-mail: ubspdbhp@sancharnet.in
No. 40/7940, Convent Road, Ernakulam-682 035
Phones: 0484-2353901, 2363905 ● Fax: 2365511
E-mail: ubspdekm@asianetindia.com
2nd floor, Apeejay Chambers, 5 Wallace Street, Fort, Mumbai-400 001
Phones: 022-56376922, 56376923 ● Fax: 56376921
E-mail: ubspdmum@mum.ubspd.com
1st floor, Halwasiya Court Annexe, 11-MG Marg, Hazratganj, Lucknow-226 001
Phones: 0522-2294134, 2611128 ● Fax: 2294133
E-mail: ubspdlko@lko.ubspd.com
680 Budhwar Peth, 2nd floor, Appa Balwant Chowk, Pune-411 002
Phone: 020-4028920 ● Fax: 020-4028921
E-mail: ubspdpune@rediffmail.com
NVK Towers, 2nd floor, 3-6-272, Himayat Nagar, Hyderabad-500 029
Phones: 040-23262572-4 ● Fax: 040-23262572
E-mail: ubspdhyd@vsnl.net
Visit us at www.ubspd.com & www.gobookshopping.com
First Published 2005

Sunil Kumar Sarkar, Director
Publishing Department, Visva-Bharati University
● 6 AJC Bose Road, Kolkata-700 017
● 2 Bankim Chatterjee Street, Kolkata-700 003
● 210 Bidhan Sarani, Kolkata-700 006
● Uttarayan, Visva-Bharati, Santiniketan-731 235

Printed at: Rajkamal Electric Press, Delhi

CONTENTS

PUBLISHER'S NOTE

Translations of Rabindranath Tagore's poems are many. So why another and why revive this already published anthology to add to the crowd?

This anthology is to be noted for its historical importance. It was for the first time in 1961 that an effort was made to introduce Tagore's major contributions to a wider readership. The Tagore Commemorative Volume Society was formed to bring out in English a selection of Tagore's work spanning areas as varied as essays on social, economic, political and educational issues and poems and songs and short stories. The society published eighteen of Rabindranath Tagore's essays in a volume entitled *Towards Universal Man*. Many scholars, thinkers, littératures and statesmen of the Western world have said that they had no idea of Tagore's insight into Indian life and how he initiated many of the creative movements of modern India till the publication of this volume.

Encouraged by the warm reception of *Towards Universal Man*, the Society took upon itself the task of preparing a companion volume in English of some of the best poems of Tagore. A large number of the poems of Tagore have already been translated into English, many of them by Tagore himself but the poems selected for translation have been of one type and were neither fully representative of nor did justice to Tagore's many-splendoured genius. Moreover, selections done by an individual translator are often coloured by personal choice. The hundred and one poems that feature in this anthology, in the opinion of the editor Humayun Kabir, represent the best of Tagore. The earliest poem in this anthology is contained in a book published in 1881 and the last poem was composed barely a week before Tagore's death in 1941. They cover an expanse of sixty years and, as the reader will see, show great imaginative sweep and energy and an amazing variety of interests. The poems have been translated by some of the most well-known names in the field of English scholarship in Bengal in the mid-twentieth century and remain some of the best available translations of Tagore's poems till date.

This work of translation done in the mid-twentieth century had long gone out of print and was not available to readers. This publication is our effort to present again before discerning readers a selection that is undoubtedly one of the foremost among the best in all available translations of Rabindranath Tagore.

ACKNOWLEDGEMENTS

Four decades ago, Humayun Kabir had brought together eighteen of the foremost literary figures of Bengal to translate some of the finest poems of Rabindranath Tagove. Some like Buddhadeva Bose, Amiya Chakravarty of Samar Sen were poets in their own right; some were renowned literary critics like Abu Sayeed Ayyub or Sisirkumar Ghose; while others were eminent educationists. But common to each one of them were their poetic sensibilities and their contribution to Tagore scholarship, qualities that have resulted in an outstanding anthology of Rabindranath's poems.

The book has long been unavailable in print and it was Moitreyee Chatterjee who had the idea of re-printing this book for present-day readers. When UBS Publishers' Distributors came up with the proposal of preparing this book afresh in collaboration with Visva-Bharati sometime in 2003, we readily agreed.

Professor Sujit Kumar Basu, Vice-Chancellor, Visva-Bharati and Professor Sudhendu Mandal, the then Director, Visva-Bharati Publishing Department (presently Director, National Library, Kolkata) saw the project through its initial stages. Professor Sabujkali Sen, Director of Culture and Cultural Relations, Visva-Bharati facilitated the publication with her timely intervention whenever necessary. Sri Nirmal Kanti Bhattacharjee, the former Director of Culture and Cultural Relations, Visva-Bharati (presently Editor, Indian Literature, Sahitya Akademi) has also been closely associated with this project.

Twenty colour reproductions of Rabindranath's paintings as also a number of manuscript pages of some of the poems included in the anthology enhances the value of this new edition. We hope it will be well received. Working to make this anthology an attractive volume have been Supriya Roy, Dilip Hazra, Asis Hazra, Sushobhan Adhikary, Santosankar Dasgupta, Samiran Nandy and Nandakishore Mukherjee, all from Rabindra Bhavana, Visva-Bharati.

Sunil Kumar Sarkar

Kolkata
January 2005

Director
VISVA-BHARATI PUBLISHING DEPARTMENT

INTRODUCTION

RABINDRANATH TAGORE is one of the outstanding literary figures of all times. In sheer quantity of work few writers can equal him. His writings include more than one thousand poems and over two thousand songs in addition to a large number of short stories, novels, dramatic works and essays on religion, education, politics and literature. In a word, his interests embrace every subject which is of interest to man. In quality, he has reached heights which have been trodden, and that too only rarely, by only the noblest among men. When one remembers the enormous range and extraordinary quality of his work, it is not surprising that his admirers should acclaim him as perhaps the greatest literary figure in history.

One can never account for the emergence of a genius, for genius is always something in the nature of an exception. It is at the same time the function of genius to find expression for the emotions and ideas which stir in the unconscious and subconscious mind of the race. A bond is thus established between the genius and his people, and helps to explain the admiration and wonder with which the genius is greeted when he appears. People find in his words and actions an embodiment of the feelings and aspirations which they have dimly felt but could not express. The genius also benefits by such relation. He derives his strength and energy from the inchoate feelings and vague aspirations stirring in the racial mind. Tagore is typical of genius in both respects. His uniqueness is beyond question and at the same time he is deeply rooted in the life of the people whom he lived for and loved.

Tagore was fortunate in both the time and the place of his birth. The advent of the West had disturbed the placid waters of Indian life and a new awakening was sweeping throughout the land. Its initial impact had dazzled the Indian mind and made many of the early reformers blind imitators of the

West. The first uncritical admiration was wearing off when Tagore was born, but the ideals brought by the West were still active and strong. At the same time, there was growing recognition of the values of India's own heritage. The time was therefore opportune for the emergence of a genius who could unite in himself Eastern and Western values.

It was not only the time but also the place which was opportune. Bengal had felt the impact of the West more vividly than perhaps any other part of India. In Bengal the new stirrings of life were most marked in Calcutta. The circumstances of his family also helped in the flowering of Tagore's genius. A pioneer of the Indian awakening, his family accepted the new challenges without giving up the rich heritage of the past. As a Brahmin, Tagore easily and naturally imbibed the traditions of ancient India and was deeply influenced not only by the literature but by the religious and cultural ideals imbedded in Sanskrit. As a member of the landed class, he was familiar with the ways of life of mediaeval India and could accept without question the composite culture of the Moghal courts. In both these respects, he was perhaps not different from other Brahmin zamindars of the day, but unlike many of them he was also sensitive to the new currents of the modern world. Steeped in the traditions of ancient and mediaeval India, his family was at the same time one of the pioneers of Western education and the Western way of life. This family background explains both the richness of Tagore's Indian heritage and the absence of any conflict or hidden stress in his mind. His was an integrated personality free from the divisions which sapped the energy of so many of his contemporaries.

Tagore was indeed fortunate that he could accept the challenge of the new without discarding the values of ancient and mediaeval India. Those who had been weaned away from their own culture and depended on the inspiration of the West lost their roots in national life. Loss of contact with the people diminished the sources of their inspiration and reduced their spiritual capital. This explains why many of them, in spite of undoubted talent and gifts, could not make a deep or abiding impact on Indian life and letters. They lacked the energy which a genius derives from its identification with the inmost urges of the race.

There is one other factor which helped Tagore in establishing his identity with the people. Quite early in life, he lived for months in a boat among the sandbanks of the *Padma* and thus came into intimate contact with the rural culture of the country. The quality of life he experienced in these regions was rooted in the primeval and ancient history of the land. Its culture goes back even deeper into the life of the people than the urban culture developed in the middle ages. Tagore thus secured an entry into a world unknown to the townsman and struck roots in some of the deepest levels of the racial consciousness. His contact with the abundant life of the common man is the source of his exuberant creative powers and explains why his inspiration never failed.

In considering Tagore's life and work, one is again and again struck by the amazing vitality of his genius. He was essentially a poet, but his interests were not confined to poetry. We have already mentioned the diversity of his literary work, but literature in its widest sense could not exhaust his energies. He was also a musician and a painter of the highest order. In addition, he made notable contributions to religious and educational thought, to politics and social reform, to moral regeneration and economic reconstruction. In fact, his achievements in these fields are so great that they mark him out as one of the makers of modern India.

Tagore's greatest strength lies in his sense of the unity of life. No bifurcation of ideals or culture divided his energies. It is therefore not surprising that he should recognise no separation between art and life. The close of the nineteenth century saw in Europe the triumph of a new aesthetic cult. There were many who held that art must be pursued for its own sake, regardless of its relation to life. The ivory tower became the symbol and type of artistic endeavour. The poet and the artist, said the votaries of this cult, were first and foremost dreamers. Tagore never accepted a conception of art divorced from life. He pursued beauty, but as a manifestation of life. Simultaneously, he held that life has no grace unless it is instinct with beauty. The religion of the poet was for Tagore also the religion of man.

II

Tagore is one of the supreme lyric poets of the world. Sincerity of feeling and vividness of imagery combine with the music of his verse to give us poems that haunt the reader long after the actual words are forgotten. This fusion of feeling, imagery and music showed very early in his life. *Nirjharer Swapnabhanga* or *The Fountain Awakes* was composed when he was barely twenty but still remains one of the supreme lyrics in Bengali, or indeed any language. The poem is remarkable not only for its music and intensity, but also for the boldness of its images. What is perhaps even more significant is the fusion of nature and man in an indissoluble unity. This identity of nature and man remained one of the most characteristic traits of Tagore's poetry throughout his life.

Perhaps there has never been another poet who loved the earth so passionately. There is hardly a single mood of day or night or of the circling seasons which Tagore has not recorded in his poetry. The sights and sounds of Bengal and especially her rural landscape are caught again and again in magic verse. Since the days of Kalidasa, Indian poets have revelled in the glories of the rainy season. Tagore has also caught the varying moods of the monsoons in a hundred songs and poems. In fact, his poems and songs of the rains have become a part of our national heritage. The expectancy of the parched earth just before the advent of the rains, the heavy smells which rise from the damp earth after the first shower, the thrill of life in the green shoots of the newly growing grass, the dark clouds which dim the clear morning light and charge with magic the evening shadows, the unceasing patter of rain in the silence of the night—these and a hundred other pictures are brought vividly to our mind in Tagore's magic verse. He has also woven into them the joys and sorrows of the human heart till nature and man reflect one another's moods and lose their separate identity.

Nor has Tagore neglected the other seasons. Autumn and spring are reflected in their many moods. The wild energy of early spring, the sense of liberation from the bonds of winter and the quick vivid burst of colour and sound are reflected in many a poem and song. They reflect not only the joyousness and strength of spring but also its sense of transience and impermanent glory. Autumn with its sense of fullness and maturity and its clear rain-washed skies has played a special role in many of Tagore's poems. One of his most successful musical plays is built round the theme of autumn with its sense of liberation from the pressure of immediate work. Even winter and summer have not been forgotten. In *Vaisakh*, one of his most famous poems, Tagore has conceived of summer as an austere ascetic who with bated breath waits for the advent of new life.

It is not only the beauty of nature that bound Tagore so intimately to the earth. He also loved the earth as the abode of man, anal has poured out his love of man in numberless poems and songs. There is hardly any feeling of the human heart to which he has not responded. The intimate play of love in all its nuances of joy and sorrow are crystallised in unforgettable words. Sorrow and anguish and the exquisite agony of hopeless waiting are reflected with a fidelity that leaves one breathless. There is also a sense of the eternal presence of nature as a companion of human emotions. He knew that life is full of strife and striving and the world is far from perfect, but he felt that the imperfections and the faults, the sufferings and longings of our earthly life make it more dear to man.

For Tagore, the world is not only a stage where man strives after a fuller life, but also a loving mother that watches over his efforts to find a richer meaning in all experience. Tagore was no ascetic and deliberately repudiated the ideal which seeks to deny the multitudinous lithe of the body. Nor was he an epicure or a hedonist, for he felt that the real glory of life lies in the constant striving for a fuller and richer experience. This yearning for fuller life recurs again and again in his poems. In *Basundhara—The World*—he sings of the abounding life of the earth and man's close kinship to the swelling tide of primeval energy. In one of his most famous lyrics, *Swarga Hoite Viday—Farewell to Heaven*—he compares the passionless calm of heavenly bliss with the exquisite flow of joy and pain in earthly experience. Tagore leaves us in no doubt where his own preference lies.

Tagore was essentially a lyric poet, but his love for nature and his sense of kinship with all life gives a rich dramatic quality to many of his poems. With his deep humanity and passionate yearning for justice, it is not surprising that he should be attracted by social and political themes. The occasion may be a particular experience, but whatever he touches is lifted to a higher plane of universal meaning. He has written some bitter satires against the prejudices and superstitions of his own people, but with a few rare exceptions, they also show how his essential humanism rises above his indignation and wrath. Even his patriotic poems are instinct with a feeling for all humanity. For Tagore, patriotism was a positive quality of love for his own people and land, never a negative attitude of hatred for the foreigner. One of the finest examples of this is seen in his poem, *Guru Govind*, where passionate love for one's country and people is seen to deepen into love for all mankind. In fact, Tagore never recognised that anything human could be foreign to him. In his famous lyric, *Prabashi (The Wanderer)*, he declares that man has his home in every clime and his country in every region of the world. This sense of identification with all mankind has found one of its finest expressions in our National Anthem where Tagore invokes the Lord of the heart of all the peoples of the world as the arbiter of India's destiny.

Tagore's love for man unconsciously and inevitably merged into love of God. We have already indicated how nature and man were united in his imaginative grasp of experience. Nor did he ever think of divinity as something apart and remote from human life. For him God was essentially love. The love of the mother for her child or of the lover for the beloved are only instances of the supreme love that is God. And this love expresses itself not only in the ecstatic devotion of the mystic but also in the routine of everyday life of the common man. Tagore repeatedly declared that God is to be realised in the common relations of life and in the daily work which sustains the world. There is no doubt that Tagore was deeply influenced by both Vaisnava poetry and Sufi mysticism. His poems and songs are full of images and themes which remind us of ecstatic experience, but we also find a keen sense of the facts of daily life. His words and phrases have an authenticity of expression that can be born only out of personal experience. Nuances of feeling are fused with moods of nature in a way which has few parallels in the world's poetry.

A word may be said about the quality of his mystic poetry. When *Gitanjali* was first published in an English translation, the West hailed it for its message of peace and love in a war-torn and embittered world. There is no doubt that the poems in that slender volume are recharged with a deep sense of peace and calm. They have an ineffable quality of beauty and remoteness in spite of the familiarity of the themes and the simplicity of the language and imagery. To readers in Europe and America, they came with the delighted wonder of a new discovery, but to readers of Tagore in Bengali the poems are only a natural culmination of his earlier writing. The love of nature and man had by unconscious steps merged into the love of God. Deep personal suffering had given a mellowness to his images and themes. Growing experience had revealed to him the undoubted truth that all our life is surrounded by mystery. The wonder and pathos of human life had brought a new sympathy and understanding to his works of imagination.

One characteristic of many of these later lyrics of Tagore is their utter simplicity. In his earlier poems, he drew largely upon the rich associations and assonance of Sanskrit. Many of them recapture the theme and spirit of classical Indian literature. He has no doubt often given a new twist to an old situation, but the affiliation with the rich mythology of India is unmistakable. In his later poems dedicated to man and God, he has shed all adornment. The simplest of human situations are used to reveal his experience of the divinity. The language also takes on the directness and simplicity of common speech. In many of these later songs and lyrics, we stand face to face with the immediacy of experience. Words have become transparent and like the notes of purest music speak to us with a vividness and force that often leave us speechless.

Nor must we forget that Tagore was throughout his life an earnest and intrepid seeker of truth. The vigour of his intellect pierced the facade of sham and hypocrisy which we often build to hide our poverty. The massive and masculine quality of his writing has remained largely unknown to those who have not read him in the original. For one thing, the translations have been selective and left out some of the most powerful examples of his intellectual sweep. For another, many of the translations are in fact adaptations and have toned down the rugged strength of the original.

The concern with man and his fate showed quite early in Tagore's life. In *Sandhya Sangeet*, one of his earliest books of poems, we already find him brooding over the problem of existence. In *Rahur Prem*, in *Chhabi O Gan*, he shows a precocious awareness of the unloveliness which results when man's selfishness masquerades as love. The philosophical strain gains in depth and intensity in *Naivedya*, but it is perhaps in *Balaka* that we have the finest fusion of intellect and emotion. Some of the poems of *Balaka* reveal an integration of thought and feeling which has transformed metaphysical speculation into the purest lyric poetry.

Tagore was reaching after new experiences and new expressions almost to the last day of his life. In his sixties, there was an outburst of lyric poetry which can compare with the best work of his early youth. The poems of this period reveal a new note of deep feeling and passion purified by suffering. The intimate and personal quality of these poems is replaced in the next decade by a rich and mellow humanism. The exuberance of his earlier writings is replaced by a rare economy of thought and expression. There is a sense of power and assurance in some of his last poems which astonish us by their intellectual vigour. There is also a new questioning of the ultimate ends of existence matched with a calm acceptance of life with all its imperfections and its promise.

III

Tagore wrote over a thousand poems and two thousand songs. He was barely fifteen when his first work was published and he wrote his last poem almost on the eve of his death. A mere statement of these facts explains why it is so difficult to make a selection of his writings. In fact, to prepare an anthology is always a difficult task. An anthology reflects the judgment of the editor and nobody can expect that his choice will satisfy all tastes. That is why we find that no anthology is ever fully satisfying. If this holds for prose, it is still truer for poetry. Different readers have their different tastes. Besides, the appeal of a poem depends on the reader's experience and mood. A poem which moves one reader may leave another cold. Even the same reader may, and does, react differently at different times and under the stress of different feelings. However skilful the selection and however conscientious the editor, it is perhaps impossible to produce an anthology which will satisfy all readers at all times.

Tagore's enormous volume, range and variety make the task of selection both more difficult and more necessary. Even the greatest of poets cannot always live on the peak of inspiration. He must occasionally relax and sometimes even descend into the valley. The average reader has neither the time nor the inclination to wade through all the writings of a master in order to discover and appreciate his finest work. Tagore's reputation has suffered with foreign readers because mainly one aspect of his writings—and that not always the strongest and the deepest—has been presented to them. This applies not only to foreign readers, but also to Indians outside Bengal. This is a national misfortune in a double sense. A majority of Indians have remained unfamiliar with some of the best writings of India's greatest poet. The world outside has been denied knowledge and appreciation of the insights achieved by one of the greatest poets of the world. It is therefore necessary in both national and international interest that a new selection of Tagore's writings should be made.

The present anthology of 101 poems is an attempt to offer to readers in English some idea of the breadth, the sweep and the vigour of Tagore's genius. Translation is one of the most difficult of arts and translation of poetry is the most difficult of all translations. As a famous poet said, poems are essentially combinations of words, and even in the same language, substitution of one word by another leads to a change in tone, atmosphere and appeal. When a poem is sought to be translated into another language, the difficulty of capturing its magic in an alien medium is inseparable. And yet, there is no alternative to making this attempt, for without translations the greatest of poets would remain unknown except only to those who share the poet's language. A translation must, from the nature of the case, be a poor substitute, but it is obviously better to have some faint idea of the beauty of a poem than to have no awareness of even its existence.

There is of course nothing sacrosanct about the number 101. If a reader says that in the case of Tagore, the number could be doubled and yet poems of only the highest quality included, I for one, would not question the statement. I would also accept the criticism that some of the poems left out of this selection are as good as if not better than those that are included. There is always room for difference of opinion as to which are the best hundred or two hundred poems of a great poet. In fact, I am keenly aware that some great poems like *Basundhara*, *Swarge Hoite Viday*, *Guru Govind*, *Prabashi* or *Tapobhanga* have been left out as they were in my view untranslatable. I would however claim for this selection two things. Nothing is included which is not first rate. Also, the selection is representative and aims at including at least some specimens of the many moods and styles in which Tagore wrote. One qualification to this statement is necessary, for songs have been left out on purpose. They no doubt include some of Tagore's finest lyrics, but songs are even more difficult to translate than poems. In their case, fusion of words and music is inviolate. Besides, Tagore himself translated a large number of songs and undoubtedly his finest English work is *Gitanjali*, an offering of songs.

The anthology starts with *Drishti* (No.1) from *Sandhya Sangeet* written when the poet was barely twenty. This is followed by *Nirjharer Swapna Bhanga* (No.2) which in Tagore's own judgment marks the awakening of his poetic genius. The lyric note struck in it is evoked again and again throughout Tagore's long creative life. Sometimes, it is tinged with a note of mystic yearning as in *Niruddesh Yatra* (No.13) or *Jivan Devata* (No.17). Sometimes, the lyric note is charged with deep human passion and significance as in *Ebar Phirao More* (No.14) or *Chhabi* (No.47). Sometimes it is a case of sheer lyricism in which sensuousness and intellectual content are fused in a perfect unity as in *Urvashi* (No.16), *Dushamaya* (No.24) or *Chanchala* (No.49).

For Tagore, man's supreme achievement lies in his conquest of private sorrow and the giant agony of the world. Man triumphs over the misery which arises out of selfishness and personal discord. He also rises above the deep sorrow that is the inescapable consequence of the transitoriness of life. In *Jete Nahi Dibo* (No.11), the poet recognises that a small child may sometimes grasp the innate truth of human nature when more sophisticated men and women fail. In *Brahman* (No.15) the teacher discovers that the dignity of man lies not in the accident of his birth, but in his acceptance of the truth without any mental reservations. In *Karna O Kunti* (No.30) and *Pratham Puja* (No.66), we have the same emphasis on the dignity of man. The pathos and the beauty of human relations are caught in smaller poems like *Didi* (No.21) or in the exquisite poems of childhood collected in *Sishu*.

Tagore has often used traditional themes and drawn extensively upon the associations and assonances of classical Indian literature. He has however transmuted whatever he has touched. Tagore had the greatest admiration for *Kalidasa*, but even when he has taken a theme from him, Tagore has given it a twist that makes his treatment essentially modern. For Tagore, *Meghdoot* (No.9) is a message not from a mythical *Yaksha* to his beloved, but an expression of the yearning of all human lovers in all ages and climes. In *Swapna* (No.25) or *Narak Bash* (No.29), he has recaptured the atmosphere of a vanished past, but he makes it clear that the past lives again in our moods and emotions of today.

Tagore experimented not only with the theme and subject but also with the form of poetry. He was never afraid of the influence of his predecessors. He borrowed freely from the traditional Vaisnava poetry of Bengal and has himself acknowledged his indebtedness to a poet like Biharilal. No man can escape his environment or his age. Attempts to do so lead more often than not to failure, and are in fact generally a symptom of the poet's lack of self-confidence. Tagore grew under the influence of contemporary society, but the very process of growth enabled him to transcend them in course of time. Once he was sure of his medium, he did not hesitate to experiment in both the form and the matter of his poetry and sought inspiration in fields of experience which had been earlier neglected in Bengali poetry. In fact, he largely obliterated the distinction between what is and what is not subject-matter for a poem. In the poems of *Kshanika*, we find him selecting themes which at first sight offer no poetic possibilities, but his genius lifts them above the level of the commonplace and makes them glow with the light of beauty. The claim of Wordsworth that the deepest experience can be expressed in the simplest terms and the facts of everyday life lit up with the light of mystery finds vivid justification in many of Tagore's poems of this period. Laughter and tears, humour and passion are fused to give a strange combination of wistfulness, yearning and mockery. We find in poems like *Jathasthan* (No.31), *Viday Reet* (No.34) or *Krishnakali* (No.33) a wonderful interplay of human moods, emotions and feelings.

Tagore was essentially a lyric genius but occasionally we find in him a sharp note of irony, if not satire, against the evils of society. He knew that the conventional Indian claim to spirituality is at times nothing but a refusal or inability to think. In *Juta Abishkar* (No.26), he has ridiculed the way in which pedantry and cant comber simple apprehension of truth. In *Devatar Grash* (No.28), he has portrayed the struggle between conventional beliefs and the religion of man and how truth ultimately prevails over the forms in which man often loses it.

Some critics may object that this anthology is overweighted with poems of his later life. There is perhaps some truth in the charge, for we have included over 40 poems written between 1927 and 1941 and less than 60 poems from the period 1881 to 1926. One reason for this is that till now, the earlier period has generally been better represented in selections in both the original Bengali and in translations into other languages. Another reason for a somewhat larger selection from the later period is that the later poems show a greater economy of thought and expression. Mastery of technique and concentration of feeling have combined to make the poems of this period deeper and more poignant. While Tagore has written many beautiful love poems in his earlier youth, they seem to play on the surface of life and do not descend into the depths where passion burns. In fact, critics have at times said that he was more concerned with words and expressions than with the experience of love. This is not quite true, for we have poems like *Ratre O Prabhate* (No.18), but if one places these earlier poems by the side of his later poetry, one has to admit that the latter has a depth and gravity which the earlier poems lack. There are few poems in any language which can match the restraint and concentrated passion of *Purnata* (No.54).

Apart from increasing intensity and concentration, the poems of his latest phase show a growing concern with the problems of the mystery of life. In spite of the great richness and variety of Bengali poetry, it has often exhibited a parochial quality. Even some of the most beautiful Vaisnava lyrics are so imbedded in local atmosphere that they cannot be lifted out of their context. One of the great achievements of Tagore was the introduction of a new note of urbanity and universality. They make his poems as appealing to a man in Europe or America as to a man in Bengal. This universal and urban note continually deepened throughout his long life and the poems of his last period show them in a most marked degree. They are also marked by the attempt at establishing a kinship with man in all his efforts and strivings, his hopes and failures, his aspirations and his daily work.

The physical suffering which Tagore had to face in his last days has been expressed in his latest poems with a vividness and poignancy that has rarely been equalled. The economy of expression in a poem like *Abasanna Chetanar* (No.82) or *Pratham Diner Surya* (No.99) is in sharp contrast with the abandon and exuberance of the poems of his early youth. Not only is there a sense of restraint and economy, but also a deep sense of fullness and completion in the last poems that he wrote. He had, it seems, made his peace with life and the world. There is misery and suffering in the world. Existence is dogged by the fact of death, but in spite of all its imperfections, life is full of significance and value. *E Dyulok Madhumaya* (No.97) is full of the sense of victory of life in the shadow of the valley of death.

It is difficult, if not impossible, to trace the development of a poet's mind. In other fields of experience there is a continuity of growth which seems to conform to certain laws. In the case of poetry, inspiration waxes and wanes in a mysterious and inexplicable manner. Some of the greatest poems of a poet have been written early in his youth while in his maturity, he often produces only mediocre or conventional work. Tagore is no exception to this rule and we find that there are exquisite poems in his earliest period and many uninspired ones in his later life. Nevertheless the way in which he sustained his inspiration throughout a long life of eighty years marks him as one of the greatest poets of all times.

Tagore summed up in himself the various strands which today make up India's composite culture. It was his special glory to catch and reflect the various aspects of India's myriad-sided life. He drew largely upon Sanskrit literature and enlarged both the vocabulary and the metric forms of Bengali. He effected an almost perfect fusion between Vaisnava lyricism and Sufi mystic feeling.

He interpreted with sympathy and imagination the courtly ways which had developed in the wake of feudalism in the middle ages. Simultaneously he drew from the untapped sources of the life of the common people. Images and symbols of the Bengal village are woven into the fabric of his poetry with exquisite skill. He also incorporated into Bengali literature the ideals and moods of Europe. The sense of power and speed in many of the poems of *Balaka* may well be derived from

European sources. Everything is transient is an ancient human finding, but Tagore gave to it a new significance by making it the symbol of the motion that is latent in all things.

In a word, Tagore's poetry is born out of an amalgam of the rich classical heritage of ancient India, the spacious ways of the Moghal court, the simple verities of the life of the common people of Bengal and the restless energy and intellectual vigour of modern Europe. He is an inheritor of all times and all culture. It is this combination of many different strands and themes that gives to his poetry its resilience, universality and infinite appeal.

Humayun Kabir
1966

THE LOOK

I wonder if your eyes learnt their twilight
 spell from the evening itself!
When you look at me, the shades of twilight
 descend on my heart and stars begin to
 shine.
Who could have guessed that such riches
 were hid in the recesses of my heart?
Now through your eyes I have seen my own
 heart.

You never sing and yet your silence teaches
 me songs: You bind my soul to the dreamy
 tranquil music of *Purabi*.

In tune with its melody I sing in loneliness
 gazing at the sky.
And the tunes reach the darkness and are lost
 in eternity!

1882
Drishti from 'Sandhya Sangeet'

1

THE FOUNTAIN AWAKES

*H*ow is it that this morning the sun's rays
   enter my very heart!
How comes it that early bird-song pierces
   today the cavern's gloom!
I do not know why, but after so very long my
   soul is awake.

My whole being surges and the waters break
   their bonds—
The heart's pain, and its passion, I can no
   longer hold in leash!

The mountain shivers in every pore and rock
   on rock rolls down.
The water foams and fumes and in pent-up
   anger roars.
Like mad, it moves in boisterous endless rings,
   rushes blindly at the dungeon-door it
   cannot see but wants to break!

Why is God so stony?
Why these barriers all around?
Awake today, my heart, and win fulfilment.
Break, break into bits the boulders in the way!
Let blow rain on blow as wave rumbles after
   wave!

When the soul is aglow, who cares for this
    rampart of gloom or the hurdle of stone?
What in the world is there to fear when the
    waters of desire overflow its shores?
I'll break this prison-house of stone and flood
    the world with the waters of compassion!
I'll pour myself out in mad fervid songs,
    flashing the bounty of my hair and weaving
    bouquets of bloom.
I'll float in the air my rainbow wings and drain
    my heart to print a smile on the fleeting
    sunbeam.

I'll rush from peak to peak, and sweep from
    hill to hill, and laugh and chant and clap
    to my own measure.
I have so much to say and to sing—my heart
    so crowded with desire and bliss.
I know not what happened today, but my
    heart is awake and from afar I hear the
    ocean's roll.
Why around me this dark prison cell?
I'll rain blow on blow and break, break, break
    its walls: for the bird-song is in my ears and
    the sunshine in my eyes!

1883
Nirjharer Swapnabhanga from 'Prabhat Sangeet'

RAHU'S LOVE

In Indian mythology Rahu is the demon who causes eclipses by swallowing the sun and the moon; although, as the result of his head having been severed from his body by one of the gods, he cannot retain his preys: symbol of frustrated desire relentlessly pursuing its object.

*E*ven though you like me not, as I have
    heard you don't, on you I shall ever hang
like an iron chain fastened to your feet.
You are the captive wretch whom my prisoner
    I have made by tying my heart to yours
    with a knot no one can undo.

Wherever on earth you go, whatever you do,
    spring or winter, day or night,
my ruthless desire will go with you like an iron
    chain clanking at your feet.
Once these eyes have seen you, you will never
    escape me.

Whether you call me or you don't
    my presence seek or shun,
I shall always be with you,—
my body merged in yours, my sorrow deep and
    dark despair;
my broken heart in your ear shrilling like a
    cracked pipe all day and night.

I shall haunt you all your life, always be your
   shadow.
My figure dark you will ever see when you
   laugh, when you cry, now in front, now
   behind, now at your side.

Alone, at dead of night, sitting up with heavy
   heart, startled, and seized with fright, you
   will see me by you seated,
my eyes on your face.
Whichever way your face you turn I shall turn
   my eyes;
wherever you look, my figure dark you will see
   painted on the sky standing between your
   world and you, concealing it from your
   view.

Like anxiety dark, I shall always surround you.
You will see my face, as in a mirror, in the tears
   you will shed.

I feel as though you and I are the only
   creatures still alive on an ocean where the
   world like a wrecked ship has sunk;
and I for life am clinging to you, while you are
   struggling to be free.

On desert sands my soul, benighted and lost, is
   ceaselessly wailing its hunger and its thirst.

Oh, to have you in my arms, and keep you
 there one livelong night!
A thirst so great as burns in me even ages will
 not allay.

Death always follows life, hope is shadowed by
 fear.
Like a *dakini** the wide world over, night is
 trailing day.
Light and shade are linked together by the
 world's decree;
so your beauty will keep alive this sateless
 hunger in me.

1884
Rahur Prem from 'Chhabi O Gan'

---

*   A hag who trails her intended victims, and calls them from behind.

6

LIFE

This world is beautiful. I do not want to die.
I wish to live in the life of man,
and have a place in his living heart,
as in a sunbright flowerful garden.
Oh, the ceaseless ripple of life on earth,
the meetings and partings so happy and sad!
With human joys and griefs I shall wreathe my
    song,
and live for ever in the deathless life of man.
If I fail, then may I have
a little place in your midst, my friends,
and make new songs at morn and eve,
like flowers that bloom to be culled by you.
    Pick my flowers with a smile on your face,
    and throw them away when they fade.

1886
Pran from 'Kari O Komal'

THE PRISONER

Take those fettering arms away,
stop those kisses like draughts of wine.
Close and stuffy is this flowery prison;
my captive heart set free, my love.
This night of full moon endless seems,
I pine for light of dawn in the sky.
Caught in meshes of your long loose hair,
from you shall I ever escape?
Your eager fingers, meeting together,
are weaving all over me a tactile net.
Whenever I open my drowsy eyes,
I see that moon with its non-stop smile.
    Take my fetters off, set me free:
    My free heart then I'll lay at your feet.

1886
Bandi from 'Kari O Komal'

VAIN DESIRE

*V*ain, these tears.
Vain, this fiery unruly desire.

The sun is about to set.
The wood is dark, the sky alight.
With slow steps and downcast eyes
Evening follows day.
Scarcely stirs the breeze,
worn with woe for parting day.

Her hands in mine, intently
I am looking into her eyes
searching for her,
wondering where she is,
where I shall find the soul
that is hidden in her.

Like the infinite luminous secret of heaven
trembling in the lonely stars
of the dusky sky,
the luminous secret of her soul
is trembling beneath the darkness deep
of her eyes.
So I am gazing into them,
and diving with all my mind and heart
into the fathomless sea of desire.

So I am striving
to know where I can find her:
within her eyes,
behind her smile,
in the sweet stream of her words,
or beneath the benign peace
that pervades her face.

Alas, my tears,
alas, my hopes too high—
not for me that joyous secret.
How rash the desire
to possess all of her.
Content I should be with what I get:
a smile, a word,
a glance,
a hint of love.

I, so poor,
what can I give in return?
Have I the endless love
that meets
the endless needs of life?
Shall I be able,
by myself,
to find the way,
and take my life-companion,
for endless days and nights,

through the boundless sky,
that holds countless worlds,
through the light and darkness deep
of myriad Milky Ways and illusory tracks,
and over the unsurmountable mountains
on which the sun rises and sets?
How could I, so timid, weary and weak,
so hungry, sad and thirsty, blind and lost,
    with heavy heart so sore afflicted—
how could I wish
to make her mine for ever?

No one belongs to us.
Human beings are not food for human hunger.
They are lotuses that bloom
for the world and its Lord—
assiduously,
and secretly.

Through days and nights
through joy and sorrow
prosperity and adversity
through life and death
and countless cycles of seasons they bloom,
to be enjoyed for their scent
and beauty and sweetness,
but not be cut
with the knife of desire.

We are to love,
and be strong in love,
but not possess our beloved:
the human soul is above human desire.

Quiet the evening, all noise hushed.
Put out with tears the fiery desire.
Slowly go back home.

November, 1887
Nisphal Kamana from 'Manashi'

ON A RAINY DAY

*O*n a day like this one could tell her.
On a day like this,
enveloped in rain and sunless,
dark and echoing with thunder.

None other shall hear.
All is lonely, all is dark.
Sit face to face, eyes looking into eyes.
The sky pours on without let,
the world seems bereft of all others.

The noises and the voices of the world
are unreal, distant, non-existent.
Only eyes drink in eyes,
only heart beats to heart.
Outside, all is merged in the dark.

Tell her, and the words will not sound rude.
Tell her, and the heart will not tremble.
Words will mingle with tears
and merge in the wind and the rain,—
One message will envelop two hearts.

What harm to any should come
if on this *Shravan* day laden with rain
I lighten my heavy heart
in this lost corner of the world?
Why, it should matter to none.

There will remain the whole of the year
for people's laughter and disdain.
Men will come and go,
there will be sorrow and pain
and life will go on for ever.
Today the wind blows restless
and lightning flashes from the sky.
Today in this pouring, deep, dark rain,
one could tell her things
that have always lurked in the mind.

May, 1889
Barshar Dine from 'Manashi'

INFINITE LOVE

*I*t seems it's you I have loved in a hundred
    forms, unending:
birth after birth, through the ages.
In many a form you have taken and swung
    around your neck the garland of songs my
    heart has stitched in sweet enchantment;
birth after birth, through the ages.

As I listen to that old-time song of pain and
    primeval love—
the old, old tale of meeting and parting—
and as I gaze into the infinite past,
at last through the darkness of Time appears
    your form like the pole-star with memories
    eternally laden.

From the heart of Time without beginning,
    we two have floated down in a double
    stream of passion.
We two have lived in a million lovers,
in the bashful smile of kissing and the tears of
    long partition,
tasting the same old love in forms for ever new.

And now that love of all the ages has met its
    last fulfilment in a heaped up offering at
    your feet.
In you are all the joys and anguish and all
    affections of the heart.
In a single love are blended the memories of
    all other passions,
and all the songs that poets have sung through
    the ages.

August, 1889
Ananta Prem from 'Manashi'

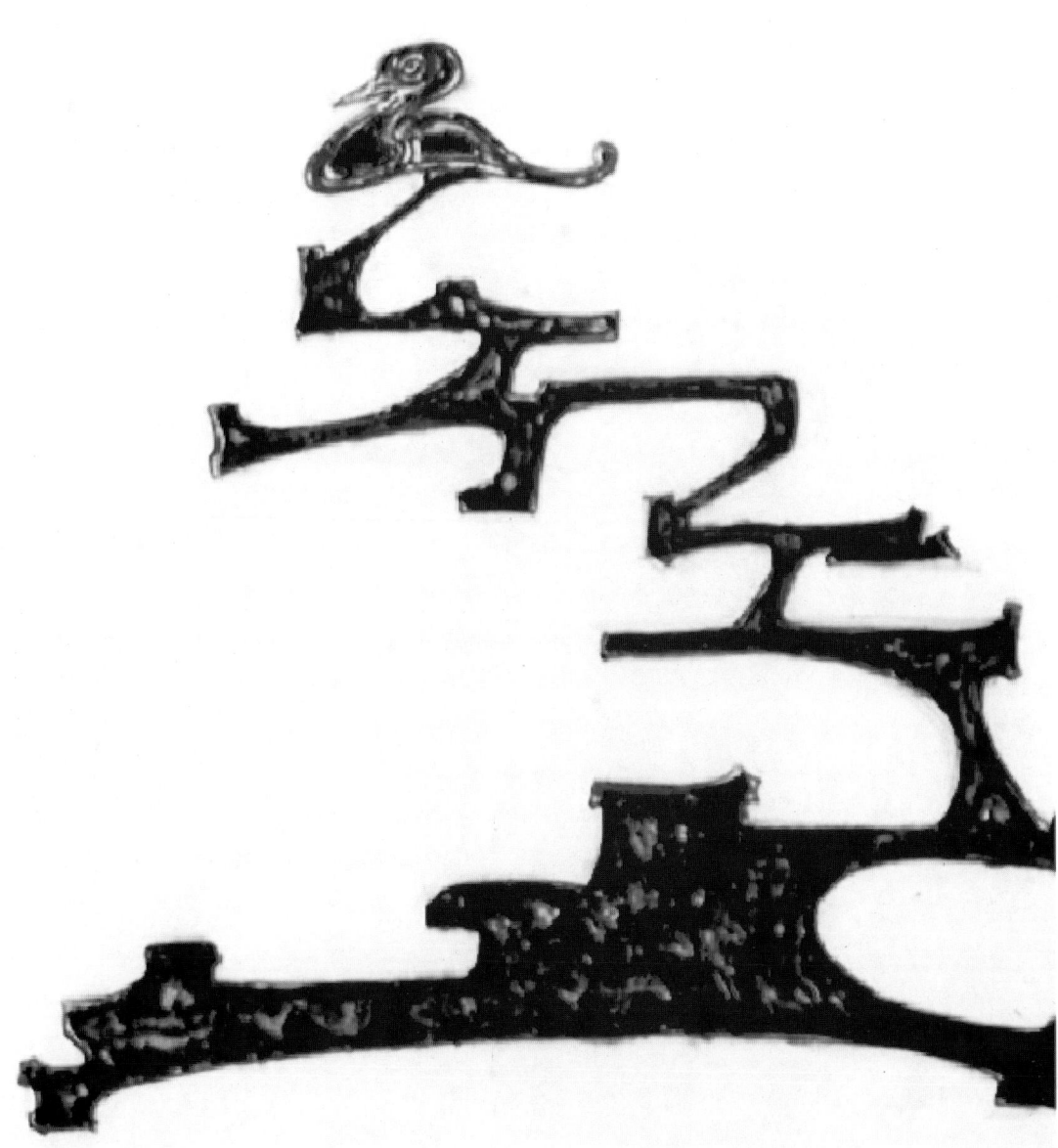

THE CLOUD-MESSENGER

*I*n which forgotten year, O Poet, did you
compose *Meghdoot* on the hallowed first day of
the rainy month of *Asadh*? Your verses,
sonorous as the rumbling clouds in their serried
darkness, stored up in the cumulus of their rich
music the sorrow of all those who were parted
from their loves.

That day, above the palace-turrets of *Ujjain*,
what an assemblage was there of clouds, what
festival of lightning, what wild rush of the wind,
what rumbles of thunder! The sombre tumult of
clashing clouds evoked at once, within a single
day, all the tearful deep-dwelling millennial cry
of the pang of separation. The pent-up sorrow of
all ages, cutting across the limits of time, poured
down unceasing, wetting with tears your noble
verses.

Did all lovers of the world who were far
from their homes sing that day in unison the
song of separation, their hands folded and their
heads lifted towards the clouds, turning in the
direction of the homes of their beloved? Did
they yearn to send on the unchained wings of
the young cloud the message of their tear-
dimmed love to those far-away casements
where the beloved lay lonesome on the floor,

her hair unkempt, her dress untidy, her eyes full of tears?

Did you, O Poet, convey their song through your music in quest of the beloved in solitude, a quest by night and day, from land to land, even as in the month of *Shravan* the river *Ganga* collects the water of far and near and flows down to lose itself in the waters of the sea; even as the *Himachal*, chained to its rocks, sees the clouds roaming freely in the sky and sadly breathes out skywards volumes of vapour from a thousand caves? Like truant desires, they rush upwards, they rise to the peak, and then they all mingle into a common shape spread over the whole sky.

A thousand times since then has the first day of the rainy season rolled by, every year have the first showers renewed the appeal of your poetry; showers that disperse the shade-giving clouds, that rouse fresh reverberations of thunder and swell the cadence of your verses like the heaving rivers of the rainy season.

How often for ages has the parted lover, of a long-drawn-out evening—an evening rain-weary, moonless and starless—sat under a lamp in a room where his beloved is not, and has read your verses to vent his own heart's aching! In your poetry resound the voices of all such men and reach me like the distant roar of sea-tide!

I am seated here in that eastern border of India, in that verdurous Bengal, where once on a rainy day the poet *Jayadeva* watched the shadows of a cloud-heavy sky on the palm-fringed horizon.

It is a dark day today; rain pours down incessantly; against the onslaught of the turbulent wind the forest cries with upraised arms. The lightning pierces through the clouds and shoots its crooked smile through the empty void.

Alone in my room, I read the *Meghdut*. Fancy-free, my mind strays; rides a cloud and flies from land to land; flies to the Mount *Amrakuta*; to the clear-streamed slender river *Reva* which flows down speed-retarding pebbles at the foot of the *Vindhya* hills; to the berry-shaded dark bank of the river *Vetravati* behind which lies hidden the village *Dasharna* fenced off with rows of the flower plant *ketaki* while the birds of the village, building nests for protection against the rains, chirp around a huge tree.

Perhaps by some river-bank there strolls a woodland girl by jasmine groves while the lily on her ear is fatigued by the heat of her cheeks

and pines for the soothing shades of clouds.
They are guileless of the art of shooting
oblique glances, these women of the
countryside whose up-gazing blue eyes reflect
the azure sky. Perhaps a maiden in a hermitage
stands entranced watching the gathering
clouds and as a sudden gale strikes her, 'God
save me, would it blow away the peak!' she
cries, she tucks up her garments and seeks the
shelter of a cave.

I fly to *Avantipuri*, to the streams that flow
out of the *Vindhyas*, to the bank of the *Sipra*
where the city of *Ujjain* gazes at the reflection
of its glory. There at midnight the doves are
asleep on palace-ledges, forgetful of
lovemaking; it is only the love-lorn woman
who goes at this hour to her clandestine tryst
along dark roads revealed momentarily by
flashes of lightning.

I wander far to *Kurukshetra*. And to *Kankhal*
where disregarding the frowns of *Gauri*, *Jahnavi*
the youthful daughter of the hermit *Jahnu*,
plays her foamy game on the moonlit plait of
hair on Shiva's head.

Thus as a cloud I wander from country to
country, arriving at length at *Alaka*, the goal of
heart's desire, where lives that archetype of
beauty, my lonesome beloved. Who but you,
O Poet, could transport me to that immortal
region, that pleasure-dome of the goddess

Lakshmi, that region of everlasting Spring
where by the ever-blossoming moonlit garden,
in the lake-skirting palace at the foot of the
blue mountains, my beloved weeps
disconsolate amidst her riches? Through the
open casement one can see her slender body
lying like a sickle moon on the bed.

The magic of your verses, O Poet, sets free
the chained agony of my heart and reaches me
to that elysium of parted love where in the
midst of perennial beauty my lonesome
beloved suffers the pang of separation night
and day.

But then the vision is lost! Around me rain
falls incessant. Desolate night approaches with
her thickening darkness. Moaning winds at the
far end of the horizon drift towards an
unknown destination.

Sleepless at midnight, I wonder whose curse
it is that parts me and my beloved! Why, my
longings retarded, should I weep with uplifted
gaze? Why should love's course be denied?

Has any man in flesh and blood ever
reached that love-lorn chamber by the lake
Manas, in a sunless gem-lit land of perpetual
twilight, at the world's end?

May, 1890
Meghdoot from 'Manashi'

TWO BIRDS

There was a bird in a cage of gold,
another free in the woods.
One knoweth not what whim of God
brought the two together on a day.
'O my friend in the cage,' said the bird from
   the woods,
'Let's together fly away to the woods'.
'Let us live quietly in the cage'
rejoined the bird in the cage.

    'Oh no', said the bird from the woods,
    'those fetters I'll never wear!'
    'Alas', the other replied,
    'I know not my way out in the woods.'

The bird from the woods sat on a bough,
and sang all the wild songs it knew.
The other said all it had learnt by rote,
the languages they spoke were different.
'Sing a song of the woods, my friend in the
   cage',
the bird from the woods was pleading;
'Learn a cage-song, please, my love from the
   woods',
was the other's importuning.

'Oh no', said the bird from the woods,
'I want no tutored rhyme',
'Alas', the other rejoined,
'I know no song of the woods!'

'The sky is blue', said the bird from the woods,
'and there is never an end to it'
'Look, how neat this cage is', the other
        replied,
'how secure on all four sides!'
'Why not let us go', said the bird from the
        woods,
'and lose ourselves among the clouds?'
'Why not' said the other 'lock ourselves safe
        in a corner of our own love-nest?'

'Oh no', said the bird from the woods,
'Where then shall I have room to fly?'
'Alas', the cage-bird sighed,
'where does one perch in the clouds?'

So it happened the birds loved each other,
but closer they could never get.
Across bars of the cage their beaks would meet
and also their silent stare.
Each failed to sense the other's state
nor why they differed so—
Lonely, they beat their wings
and plaintively called one to the other.

'Oh no', said the bird from the woods,
'the cage door might shut me in'.
'Alas', the cage-bird moaned,
'I haven't the strength to fly!'

July, 1892
Dui Pakhi from 'Sonar Taree'

'I WILL NOT LET YOU GO'

The carriage waits at the door. It is now
    midday.
The autumn sun is getting more and more
    intense.
Midday gusts waft the dust across the deserted
    village path.
An old beggar woman has spread her rags in
    tired slumber beneath the cool shade of the
    banyan tree.
On all sides stretches a sun-flooded night void
    of speech or sound or sign of life.
Only in my house there is no trace of rest
    or sleep.

II

Aswin is over and my autumnal holidays are
    ended.
I must return to my distant place of work
    again.
Busy servants flit about with cords and ropes,
    call one another from room to room and tie
    up many packs.
My wife with grief-laden heart and tear-
    dimmed eyes lacks leisure even to
    weep alone.

দুপারে প্রস্তুত গাড়ি; বেলা দ্বিপ্রহর;
শরতের রৌদ্র ক্রমে হতেছে প্রখর;
জন...শ্রীঘৃণ্য ভূমি উর্দ্ধ যায়
মধ্যাহ্নে বাতাসে; শুভ্র আকাশে হৃদি
ক্লান্ত...ভিখারিণী — একটি কীর্ণ ... গাড়ি
ছুমায়... সংক্ষেপে; যেন বৌদ্ধমঠী গাড়ি
ধীরে ধীরে করে চারিদিকে, নিষ্ক্রম ভিক্ষুমঠ —
— ও হু! মোর ঘরে নাহি বিশ্রামের সুখ!

শিশুকে আগলিন, — সুঘার ভূমির শেষে
ফিরে এসে হার আমি ওই দূর দেশে
সেই কর্মস্থলে। দূঢ়/সকল ব্যস্ত হয়ে
কাঁহিয়ে নিশ্চিত করে মৃন্ময়...এসে
হাঁকরি হাঁকরি সংকোচি এ ঘরে ও ঘরে
ঘরে সুস্বিনী, — দূর দূর করে —
... করে সাদালার ভয়, —
তবু মনে চায় নাহি কাঁদিবার
ভয়; — বিদায়ের আয়োজনে
এসে হয় সিন্ধুর মায়ার না হয় মরণ

She bustles about to make sure I have all
    I need.
However much the luggage grows, she is not
    content.
In despair I ask, 'What do you intend?
What shall I do with all this wealth of a king's
    household,
with so many jugs and pots and plates
    and bottles and beds and boxes?
Let me leave behind some and take some
    with me.'

III

No one pays any attention to what I say.
'Who knows—if suddenly you need them in
    an alien land
where will you find these things?
Pulses like gold and rice of the finest grain,
areca nuts and betel leaves are there.
Some jaggery cakes I have put in that
    covered dish.
Here are some coconuts, there two jugs of
    mustard oil,
mango pan-cakes, mango dried and two seers
    of milk.
Here are bottles full of medicine, and there
    some sweets.

Swear that you won't forget to eat them on
  the way.'
I knew all argument or reason was vain.
The luggage piled up like a very mountain.
I looked at the watch and looked at the dear
  dear face.
Slowly I said, 'Now I must go.'
She turned her face and pulled her scarf over
  lowered eyes to hide her tears lest they do
  me harm.

IV

My four year old daughter sat absent-minded
  by the door.
On other days she would, by now,
  have bathed
and gone off to sleep with scarce
  half-finished meal.
Today her mother could not attend to her.
Though it was late, she was neither bathed
  nor fed.
So long she had shadowed me and watched in
  attentive silence all I did.
Now, with tired limbs she sat quietly by
  the door and none knew what was on
  her mind.
I spoke to her, 'Little mother mine, good bye'.

With sad eyes and solemn face, she said,
    'I will not let you go'.
She kept on sitting where she was,
she did not cling to me nor seek to block
    the door,
With love's assurance she only said
    'I will not let you go',
        but it was time to go and alas! I went.

V

Who art thou, my foolish girl?
Where didst thou find the strength to say
    words so bold and proud: 'I will not let
    you go'?
Whom wilt thou hold in the fleeting world
    with thy tiny hands, proud maid?
Wilt thou sit with tired limbs by the
    homestead door and fight the forces of the
    world with the force of love alone?
Our hearts are full of grief and yet all that we
    can say is expression of a timid hope,
'We want that you should stay'.
Who is there that dares to say:
    'I will not let you go'?
Thy infant lips voiced the proud claim of love.
The world laughed at thee and dragged me off.
With defeated eyes thou satst by the door like
    a sad picture in a frame.
I looked at thee and left with tearful eyes.

VI

I went along my way.
On both sides of the road
I saw the autumn fields weighed with corn and
    basking in the sun.
The rows of trees stand desolate by the road
    and all day long gaze at their own shadow.
The Ganges flows to sea in full autumnal flood.
White strips of cloud lie upon the azure sky,
like new-born calves sleeping after a feed of
    mother's milk.
The age-old earth is bare in the bright
    sunlight and stretches to the far horizon.
I looked at her tired stretch and a deep sigh
    welled up from my heart.

VII

What sombre sadness broods over earth
    and sky.
Far as I go, I hear one monotonous wail, one
    melancholy note: 'I will not let you go'.
From the earth's rim to the farthest horizon
    there echoes the endless cry:
    'I will not let you go'.
A mere wisp of grass, but Mother Earth
    clings to it, hugs it to her heart and cries,
    'I will not let you go'.

A flame flickers in the dying lamp.
Before darkness can envelop it, there rings a
     cry, 'I will not let you go'.
Throughout heaven and earth's boundless
     stretch, it is the oldest cry, the deepest wail,
     'I will not let you go'.
And yet all things go and we must let
     them go!
This has been since the flow of time began.
Creation's currents sweep to Destruction's sea.
We stretch out eager arms, our eyes glow with
     hope, we proclaim, 'I will not let you go'.
And yet all are swept by the resistless flood.
In vain we fill the shores of time with sad
     lament.
The wave behind calls to the forward waves,
     'I will not let you go'.
No one listens to the call and no one heeds.

VIII

I heard voiced the sad lamenting wail welling
     from the heart of the universe in my little
     daughter's words.
From every side arose the same unreasoning
     claim in unceasing notes.

The earth ever loses what she gets but will not
    loose her hold, will, like my little daughter
    four years old, declare in the pride of love,
    'I will not let you go'.
Pale of face and eyes dim with tears every day
    and hour her hopes are rudely blown and
    yet Love will not know defeat, will still
    declare in defiant tones,
    'I will not let you go'.
Every time she tastes defeat she says,
'How can he I love go away from me?
What's there so strong or boundless as my
    desire?'

Love declares in pride of inner strength,
    'I will not let you go'.
But alas! Like dry dust wafted by the
    idle breeze,
Love sees the beloved borne away by flow
    of time.
Her eyes are washed with tears, with broken
    heart she crumbles down to earth, and still
    insists, 'God will not break His troth.
He has promised Love eternal mastery.'
Love with her slender grace boldly faces
    Death, stands before his overpowering
    might and denies the very fact of death.

Love's proud words make Death laugh, but she
     suffers death and yet for ever lives,
     permeates the vastness of the universe even
     while she trembles in anxious fear like a veil
     of tears on sad solemn eyes.
The heart keeps fighting against the loss of
     hope, and spreads a pall of sadness
     o'er the world.
I look inward and I see:
Two unreasoning arms that hold in vain
     embrace the dumb and painful earth.
A steady shadow broods over the
     moving waters.
Is it the shadow of a cloud full of tears?

                        IX

I hear a voice of yearning in the rustle of
     the trees.
In idle indifference the warm midday wind
     plays with the dead dry leaves.
Slowly, the day wanes and the shadows
     lengthen beneath the *Aswatha* tree.
The infinite plays a sad rustic pipe across the
     plains of the world.
The earth listens to the tune.

With loosened hair falling o'er her neck and a
　　golden scarf that gleams in the yellow sun
　　flung across her breasts, she sits in the vast
　　fields of corn by the river-side.

Her steady eyes gaze at the distance.
Her voice is mute with speechless silence.
I look at her sad solemn face, and it is the face
　　of my four year old daughter as she sat
　　brooding by the door.

October, 1892
Jete Nahi Dibo from 'Sonar Taree'

34

MY HEART IS LIKE A RIVER

*I*f you would fill your pitcher
come down here, into the river of my heart.
The deep water will weep and ripples whisper
around your gentle feet.
In the depths of the monsoon lies the day.
Clouds trail along my banks like dark tresses.
Ankle-bells tinkle; footsteps advance;
Who comes, all alone, to the banks of
    the river?
If you would fill your pitcher
come down here, into the river of my heart.

If you would rather sit on the shore
and let the pitcher float away on the water,
here you will find grass as velvet,
cool forests glistening with flowers
under a dark blue sky.
Through two dark eyes the mind will wander,
robes will slip down unheeded,
memories will stir as you sit on the soft grass
by the river bank and look at the
    flowering trees.
If you would rather sit on the shore,
let the pitcher float away on the water.

If you would rather bathe,
come down here into the dark still water.

No need for your sky-blue skirt, leave it on
    the shore.
The blue water will hide your nakedness,
waves in rapture will break upon your body,
and rush to caress your throat and breasts.
Ripples will laugh and cry and encircle you
and whisper secrets into your ears.
If you would rather bathe,
come down here into the dark still water.
If you would rather die,
Plunge here into the deep water.
Cold, fathomless and calm,
the still blue water is gentle as death.
Here there is neither day nor night,
the end is lost and so the beginning,
no music is heard, nor voices.
Lost to everything, free of all bonds,
leave on the shore the trammels of work.
If you would rather die,
Plunge here, into the depths.

June, 1893
Hriday Yamuna from 'Sonar Taree'

DESTINATION UNKNOWN

*H*ow much farther will you lead me on, Lady
    beautiful?
Tell me where will finally land your golden
    boat?
Whenever I ask you, Lady of far-off land,
you only flash at me your dulcet smile.
I do not know what thoughts stir in your
    mind.
Silently you lift your finger
and point to the infinite sea which heaves.
In the far west the sun hides behind the sky.
What lies there? What is it we go to seek?

Tell me, I once again ask you Lady unknown:
On the evening sands burns the day's funeral
    pyre,
the waters shine like liquid fire,
the sky melts down in limpid flow,
the eyes of the horizon swim in tears.
Do you have your dwelling there
beyond the wave-studded sea?
At the foot of the cloud-kissed western hills?
You smile silently but say no word.

The wind moans day and night with
    longdrawn sighs.
The waters swell and roar in blind agony.
The dark blue waters are full of doubts.

There is no trace of shore on any side.
An endless weeping sweeps through the world.
On the sea of tears floats the golden boat.
The evening sun strikes it with golden shafts.
Why in its centre you sit and smile silently?
I do not understand what stirs in your mind.

When first you asked who will come with you,
I looked into your eyes in the early dawn.
You pointed with lifted finger
to the infinite sky that stretches west,
the restless light that flickers on the waves
    like hope.
I boarded the boat and asked,
'Shall we find new life there beyond?
Does hope yield there its golden harvest?'
You looked at my face and smiled without
    a word.

Since then we sometimes saw the sun and
    sometimes clouds.
Sometimes the sea was rough and
    sometimes calm.
Time flows on and the wind strikes the sails.
The golden boat moves blithely forward.
Now the sun descends in the western sky.
Once again I ask you, Lady of mystery,
Is cool death to be found there beyond?

Is there peace, is there sleep in the depths of
the dark?
Again you lift your eyes and smile silently.

Soon the dark night will spread her wings.
The golden light will be lost in the evening
sky.
Your body's fragrance comes floating in the air,
in my ears there is the murmur of moving
waters,
your hair flies in the wind and touches my
face.
With faint heart and tired frame,
once again I shall ask you impatiently,
'Where are you? Come and touch me once'.
You will say no word and I shall not see your
silent smile.

December, 1893
Niruddesh Yatra from 'Sonar Taree'

CALL ME BACK TO WORK

*W*hile the world was busy with a
    hundred chores,
you played O Poet upon your flute the
    livelong day
like a truant boy who has fled from home:
alone in the fields under the sad shade of trees,
the hot midday wind heavy with distant
    forest scents.

Shake off your sleep and rise.
There is fire around.
Who blows the conch to wake the people of
    the world?
Whence come the wails that resound in
    the sky?
From what dark dungeon do forsaken women
    cry for help?

Bloated insolence with million snouts
sucks the heart-blood of the weak.
Proud injustice mock at pain.
The cringing slaves hide in borrowed robes.
They stand dumb with heads bent low.
On their face is writ the age-old tale of woe.
Toiling under mounting loads
they drag their steps and slowly march
till the last breath of life

and then hand down the burden to their heirs.
They do not revile their fate nor curse
   their God,
they blame no man, they know no pride,
they only seek to live their dreary life
by picking crumbs of food.
When these crumbs are snatched away,
when blind insolence strikes with cruel blows,
they know not where to seek redress.
One long sigh rises towards the poor
   man's God
and then they die in silence.

II

We must bring speech to these dumb
   denuded lips.
We must light with hope these weary
   empty hearts,
we must call to them and say:
'Hold your heads high and together stand.
The wrong-doer whom you fear is more afraid
   than you
and will flee in haste if you challenge him.
If you face him with dauntless heart
he will slink away in fear and shame
like a cringing cur.
Accursed of God and bereft of friends,
he brags loudly but in his heart of hearts
he knows his utter emptiness.'

Gather yourself, O Poet and arise.
If you have courage, bring it as your gift.
There is so much sorrow and pain,
a world of suffering lies ahead—
poor, empty, small, confined and dark.
We need food and life, light and air,
strength and health and spirit bright with joy
and wide bold hearts.
Into the misery of this world, O Poet,
bring once more from heaven the light of faith.

III

I appeal to thee, Imagination full of wiles,
call me back to the world's firm shore.
Waft me not from wind to wind,
nor toss me from wave to wave.
Do not make me forget through magic charm,
nor keep me in restful idleness
in the cool shade of my heart
dark with sadness and solitude.
The day ebbs and evening deepens.
Darkness covers all sides.
The forest moans in a long drawn sigh
in the desolate wail of the wind.

I came out and stood under the open sky
on the wide dusty highway amidst the crowd.
Where do you go traveller, where?
I am a stranger, look at me.

Tell me your name,
do not regard me with distrust.
For ages have I lived alone
in my own strange world of day and night,—
hence my alien dress, my exotic ways.
That is why my eyes are full of dreams
and my heart of hunger.
What strange Mother handed me an idle Flute
the day I was born into this world?

Swept away by the music I made myself
I travelled through long days and nights
beyond the world into regions far-away.
If the joy of the music I have learnt
can fill the mansions of this world
—void of song and full of tiredness—
with the note of hope that conquers death,
if I for a moment can
disturb the torpor of this workless life,
if sorrow finds its speech,
if the deep yearnings of the heart awake
and reach out for the light of heaven,
then alone will my song be sanctified,
and find in resplendent music
fulfilment for all disappointments of life.

IV

Marching with the waves of Life Eternal
we must go forward with Truth as our
        Polar Star
and no thought of death.
Inclement evil days will pour upon our heads,
but we must struggle on
to keep our Tryst with Him
at whose feet we poured the riches of our heart
from age to age.

Who is He?
We do not know and have never known.
This alone we know that through the
        darkest night
it is to Him that men go travelling on
through storm and thunder
throughout the ages long
guarding with care the flame that burns
        in them.

Only this we know that who have heard
        His call
have gone forward with fearless heart
and endured torture with patient calm.
In the whirl of danger they have poured
        their all,—

the voice of death has been music to
    their ears.
They have faced the flames, suffered at
    the stake,
and been hacked with sword,
but with unflinching heart
have lit the sacred fire
and brought all dear belongings to
    the sacrifice,
with their last breath have worshipped Him
and found fulfilment in death.

We have heard,
for Him the Prince has left his realm
and come out a beggar in tattered rags.
Great hearts have endured from day to day
pinpricks of daily life.
Thorns have pierced their feet,
the worldly wise have mocked at them,
friends have poured out cold contempt.
They have forgiven all
with silent benediction in their eyes.
The mighty have placed their honour at
    his feet,
the rich their wealth, heroes their lives.
Poets have made a million songs
and scattered them through the world.

We only know
that for the sake of Universal Love
we must sacrifice all pettiness,
discard all indignity to life,
and stand up with lifted head,
unscarred by fear and unmarked with
    slavery's badge.

March, 1894
Ebar Phirao More from 'Chitra'

The first three sections of the poem have been translated recently and conform as closely as possible to the original. The fourth section, based on a version approved by the poet and published in the Visva-Bharati, Vol. VIII No. 1 (July 1939) is *not* a literal translation.

BRAHMAN

*I*t was evening, the sun had just set and on the *Saraswati's* banks, the forest shadows had darkened. To the silent *ashram* returned the children of the sages, on their heads small loads of sacrificial log collected in nearby woods. Called back from daylong pasture, the *ashram* cattle browsed calmly, tired, yet their eyes tranquil with content. A knot of young people, freshly bathed, sat in the open space before the hut, circling round Gautam, their *guru*. The darkness was lit by the embers of the sacrificial fire. Above, in the heaven's immensity, a great peace ruled sunk in thought. The stars in rows stood quiet and curious like expectant pupils. Silence broke, as Gautam's voice rang softly: 'Listen carefully my children, for I shall tell you of *Brahman*, the knowledge of Reality.'

It was then that a young lad came into the compound, holding in both hands a casket of flowers and fruit. He placed it devoutly at the sage's lotus feet, and bowing profoundly, spoke in ambrosial voice that the cuckoo could envy: 'Sire, I am *Satyakama*, from Kurukshetra. Desirous of initiation at your hands, I wish to learn the truth about *Brahman*.'

The great sage smiled. 'May your path be smooth', he said, his voice full of the quietude

47

of compassion, 'Tell me your clan, my child,
for *Brahmins* alone have the right to such
study.' Slowly, the lad made reply: 'I do not,
sire, know my clan; let me ask mother and I'll
tell you tomorrow.'

Bowing again at the sage's feet, the boy
walked back along the dark forest paths,
crossing on foot the thin opaque and restful
Saraswati—back to his mother's cottage by the
sand, where the sleeping hamlet ended.

The evening lamp flickered dimly, as his
mother Javala stood by the door, anxiously
awaiting her child's return. She drew him to
her and kissed his head, murmuring words of
benediction. 'Tell me, mother,' he asked:
'What is my father's name? And our clan? To
the sage Gautam I went and begged initiation
as his pupil. Only Brahmins he said had the
right. What is my clan, mother?'

Her face lowered, his mother softly said,
'When I was young and very poor, I served
many masters and you came into my lap. You
are the son of Javala who had no husband.
You are my child, but your clan I know not.'

Morning came. Dawn, fresh and benign,
wakened the tree-tops. The sage's disciples
matched the young light's dewy radiance,
emitting as it were the luminousness of virtue
cleansed in the tears of devotion. Straight from
morning ablutions, their matted hair still

dripping, they sat around Gautam in the shade
of the aged banyan, Gautam whose presence
was an effulgence of beauteous purity. Birds
and honey bees and the running stream made
a concord of sound, grave and sweet, as many
young throats chanted Vedic verse.

Slowly came Satyakama, bowing low at the
sage's feet, and sat, without a word, his large
eyes unclouded. The sage gave him his
blessings and asked: 'What is your clan, my
serene and comely child?' 'Sire', said the boy,
his head upraised, 'I do not know, but I asked
my mother. She said she did not know either,
for she had served many masters, and I was
born in the lap of Javala who had no
husband.'

The strange tidings stunned all. Like bees
scattered by a blow on a honey-hive, they
hummed in agitation. Some laughed in
derision, some cursed the arrogance of the
shameless outcaste. Only Gautam rose, his
arms open. Hugging the boy to his heart, he
said: 'You are not beyond the pale, my child.
You're the best of Brahmins for you are born to
Truth!'

February, 1895
Brahman from 'Chitra'

URVASHI

In Indian mythology Urvashi arose from the primeval ocean when it was churned by the gods and the demons. She became the principal dancer before the gods in heaven, and was sometimes sent by them to disturb the meditation of men who tried to become godlike by the acquisition of spiritual power. She is the ideal of beauty, the unattached spirit of love and life ever dancing in the universe.

*N*either mother nor daughter nor wife
    are you,
O celestial Urvashi!
In no home do you light the lamp, when
    Evening
On the pastures alights, wearily holding her
    golden skirt.
With halting steps, with throbbing breast and
    downcast eyes,
To no bridal bed you smiling shyly go
In silent midnight.
Unabashed you are, and, like the rising dawn,
Unveiled.

A stemless, self-blown flower,
When did you blossom, Urvashi?
That primal spring morn, when from the
    churned ocean you rose,
Nectar in your right hand, poison in your left,
The billowy deep, like a serpent charmed
    with spells,
Lowered its million swollen hoods,
And fell at your feet,

50

As jasmine-white and naked you rose,
    a paragon
By heaven's king adored.

Were you ever bud, ever child of tender age,
O eternally youthful Urvashi!
In what father's home in the dark ocean cave
The lonely child with pearls and jewels played?
On coral bed in pearl-lit chamber,
Lulled by the sea-waves' drowsy song,
In what mother's arms sweetly smiling,
She fell asleep?
Youthful you were when on earth you rose,
A full-blown flower.

In every age the world's dearest love,
O wondrously beautiful Urvashi!
Ascetics their meditation break, its fruit at your
    feet to lay;
At the glance of your eyes the world with
    youth grows restless;
The blinded winds your intoxicating fragrance
    waft around;
The raptured poet seeks you like the honey-
    mad bee the flower,
With overflowing song,
As tinkling *nupuras** and waving skirts you go,
Quick as lightning.

---

* Ankle-bells worn by Indian dancers.

In the assembly of the gods when you dance in
    ecstasy of joy,
O swaying wave, Urvashi!
The sea surges in the same rhythmic dance;
In the crests of the corn the skirt of the earth
    shivers;
From the jewelry on your breasts stars drop
    into the sky.
Suddenly in the breast of man the heart loses
    itself,
The blood-stream dances.
Suddenly on the horizon your girdle bursts
    asunder;
O wild abandon!

Dawn incarnate on eastern mount of heaven,
O world-bewitching Urvashi!
Your slender limbs are bathed in the tears of
    the world,
Your feet are red with the blood of its heart.
Loose-haired and naked, on the centre
Of the blossomed lotus of the world's desire
Lightly you rest your feet.
Infinite are the roles you dance in the mind's
    infinite heaven,
O visitant in dreams!
Do you not hear the world crying for you,
O Urvashi, cruel and deaf!
Crying for the return of that ancient
    primal age,

When from the boundless ocean's depths,
    wet-haired
As on that primal morn, you will rise again.
Stricken with the world's gaze, all your limbs
    will weep,
Dripping brine,
And suddenly the mighty waters will surge
    with a song
Unsung before.

For ever is gone that prime. On the western
    mount are you set,
O glorious moon, Urvashi!
So on earth today the joyous breath of spring
Is mixed with the sigh of a separation long.
On night of full moon, when earth with
laughter brims,
Dim memory flutes a far-off aching tune,
And tears flow.
To hold you by that aching heart the world
    still hopes,
Free though you are.

December, 1895
Urvashi from 'Chitra'

LORD OF MY LIFE

My heart's inmost One,
are your desires quenched having come to my
    heart?
With myriad streams of sorrow and joy
your cup I have filled
crushing with harshness my heart even as
    grapes are pressed.
Of such colour, such fragrance,
such melody, such rhythms
threading one upon another, I have made your
    wedding bed:
melting passion's gold
for your fleeting play fashioned images eternally new.

With what hope you chose me I do not know.
Lord of Life,
have you found delight, where you dwell
    alone,
in my nights and mornings
my pleasures, my work?
In Rain, in Autumn, in Spring and in Winter
when songs resound in my heart,
did you hear them where you sit solitary upon
    your throne?
Did you gather the flowers of my mind,
weave them into a garland wear them about
    your neck,
and traverse the forest of my youth at your will?

Friend, looking deep into my being
did you forgive my lapses, my falls, my errors?
The worshipless day, the night without
    service—
they came and went, my Lord,
the flowers for offering blossomed and fell in
    the garden.
My *Veena's* string which you set to music
slackened time and again—
O Poet, how could I sing the song of your creation?
While watering your garden, I fell asleep in the
    shade,
and came in the evening, my eyes filled with tears.
Has it ended now, my Lord, all that was mine—
the beauty, the song, the life, the waking hours
    and the drowsiness of sleep?

The bondage of my arms is loosened,
my kisses have lost their wine—
has the night of tryst in life's arbour now paled
    into dawn?
Break, then, this meeting of today,
bring new forms, new grace,
take me and shape me who is ever-old,
bind me in our marriage in the new life.

February, 1896
Jivan Devata from 'Chitra'

LAST NIGHT AND THIS MORNING

*L*ast night in the enchantment of the
    moonlit bower
I held up the brimful cup of youth to your lips.
Gazing intently into my eyes,
slowly you took it from my hand,
and with lips moist with kisses, smiled
    and drank.
Last night in the moonlight, in the
    enchanted hour.

I drew away your veil;
I seized your lotus hands
and held them against my heart.
Your eyes drooping with the weight of love,
your lips were silent in ecstasy.
I unfastened your hair
and let it stream down your face
and rested your shyly lowered head on
    my breast.
You bore all my caresses with a rapt smile,
last night, in the moonlight, in the
    enchanted hour.

This morning, in the cool breeze of the lonely
    riverside
in white robes, just-bathed, slowly you walk,
gently holding the wicker basket,
    picking flowers.

From far off temples come the melodies
  of dawn
across the pure air of the cool morning on the
  banks of the Ganga.
Fresh vermilion in the parting of your hair,
Pure white conch-shell bangle on your arm,
Goddess-like you shine, in the light of
  the dawn.
Last night you came, my love, as mistress of
  my heart,
today you stand before me a smiling Goddess.
I stand in the distance, filled with awe
in the pure light of this cool dawn by the
  lonely riverside.

February, 1896
Ratre O Prabhate from 'Chitra'

57

1996

*W*ho are you reading curiously this poem
     of mine
a hundred years from now?
Shall I be able to send to you
—steeped in the love of my heart—
the faintest touch of this spring morning's joy,
the scent of a flower,
a bird-song's note,
a spark of today's blaze of colour
a hundred years from now?

Yet, for once, open your window on the south
and from your balcony
gaze at the far horizon.
Then, sinking deep in fancy
think of the ecstasies of joy
that came floating down
from some far heaven of bliss
to touch the heart of the world
a hundred years ago;
think of the young spring day
wild, impetuous and free;
and of the south wind
—fragrant with the pollen of flowers—
rushing on restless wings to paint the earth
with the radiant hues of youth
a hundred years before your day.

And think, how his heart aflame,
his whole being rapt in song,
a poet was awake that day
to unfold like flowers
his myriad thoughts
with what wealth of love!—
one morning a hundred years ago.

A hundred years from now
who is the new poet singing his songs to you?
Across the years I send him
the joyous greeting of this spring.
May my song echo for a while,
on your spring day,
in the beating of your heart,
in the murmur of bees,
in the rustling of leaves,—
a hundred years from today.

February, 1896
1400 Shan from 'Chitra'

RENUNCIATION

*H*e said at midnight, he who had lost relish
  for worldliness,
'I leave home tonight for the sake of my Lord,
but who is it that holds me back with guile?'
—'I', said the Lord, but the man had no ear
  for the voice.

There on the edge of their bed, hugging her
  baby to her breast,
sleeps his darling wife in peace.
'Who are you', he cried, 'playing tricks of
  illusion on me?'
—'I', said the Lord, but the man would pay
  no heed.

He left his bed and cried, 'Where art thou, my
  God, my God!'
—'Here', said the Lord but he would not hear.
The child cried in a dream and clung to the
  mother.
'Come back', said the Lord but he would not
  respond.

'Alas!' sighed God,
'Where does my worshipper go leaving me behind?'

March, 1896
Bairagya from 'Chaitali'

60

SISTER

West-country labourers are digging up earth for a kiln by the river.

The young daughter of one of them comes daily to the ghat* to scour pots and pans. She comes running, her brass bracelets tinkling on the brass utensils. She is very busy, almost bent under the weight of work, all day.

Her little brother, shaven, muddy and naked, follows her like a tame animal; sits down on the high bank as she tells him, and waits with quiet patience for her work to be over.

She leaves for home with a full pitcher on her head, plates on her left hip, and her brother's hand in her right hand.

The sister, herself a child is also a mother in their mother's absence.

April, 1896
Didi from 'Chaitali'

---

* *ghat* : Landing stage.

THE INTRODUCTION

*O*ne day I saw the naked boy sitting in the
dust with stretched legs, while his sister was in
the ghat, scouring a bowl round and round
with lumps of earth.

A soft-coated kid, that had been browsing
on the bank, suddenly came near the boy, and
after looking at him awhile, gave a bleat.

Startled, and trembling with fear, the boy
cried aloud.

Dropping the bowl, the sister came up
running. She took the boy in one arm; the kid
in the other, and caressed them both alike.

Introduced to each other this way, the
human child and the animal child became
friends.

April, 1896
Parichaya from 'Chaitali'

62

FIRST KISS

The skies lowered their eyes and grew silent.
The birds ceased to sing.
The wind dropped, rippling waters stilled at
    once and forest murmurs faded in the heart
    of the forest.
The horizon came down on the silent earth
    along the lonely bank of the silent river in
    the still shadow of the evening.
At that instant, at the solitary silent window
    we kissed each other for the first time.
All at once evening bells rang out in the
    temple and filled the sky.
The eternal stars shivered and our eyes filled
    with tears.

July, 1897
Pratham Chumban from 'Chaitali'

BAD TIMES

*T*hough evening comes with slow weary steps
and all song is stilled at a hint,
though the endless skies stretch, lonely,
and weariness descends on every limb,
though a great fear counts its silent beads,
and the face of the horizon is veiled,
Yet, O bird, mine bird,
do not, sightless, furl your wings!

Here isn't the hum of murmuring woods,
but the sea-swell roaring with the
    serpent's rage.
Here isn't a bower tinted with *Kunda* blossom,
but the restless surge of loud, rollicking foam!
O where is the coast where flowers and twigs
    entangle?
O where is the nest, the sheltering bough?
Yet, O bird, mine bird,
do not, sightless, furl your wings!

Still stretches ahead the lengthening night,
and the sun sleeps in the distant sunset hill.
Stockstill and with bated breath the world
keeps lonely vigil as the moments glide.
There, in the far sky, floats a pale moon,
sickle-thin, swimming out of the deeps of gloom.
O bird, mine bird,
do not, sightless, furl your wings!

High in the sky the stars stare down,
fingers outstretched, their glances backoning.
Far below, in a hundred waves,
Death rushes in tumult, heedless and grave.
'Come, O come!' call anxious voices,
from far away, heavy with pity and pleading.
O bird, mine bird,
do not, sightless, furl your wings!

No, there's neither fear nor the binding fancies
    of love,
there is no hope, for hope is plain deceit,
there isn't the wangle of words and vain
    crying,
there isn't home nor floral bedecking.
Only these wings are there and the sky's
    boundless realms
dawn-abandoned, hued with deep gloom
O bird, mine bird,
Do not, sightless, furl your wings!

April, 1897
Dushamaya from 'Kalpana'

65

THE DREAM

$\mathcal{F}$ar, far away, at the dream-city of *Ujjain*, by
the bank of the river *Sipra*, I go searching for
my beloved of a former birth:

Her face pollen-powdered, a pink lotus in
her hand, white lotus buds stuck behind her
ears, and crimson amaranth in her hair; her
lithe body enwrapped in a crimson *sari*, her
anklets tinkle shyly.

On a day of Spring-time, I tread far and
wide along a half-remembered way.

In the great temple of *Mahakal*, resonant
bells toll at the hour of evening worship.

The market place is deserted, and one can
see the beams of the setting sun beyond the
high darkling roofs.

Here's my beloved's house at the end of the
winding, narrow and lonesome road.

On the doors are painted emblems of conch
and wheels and on both sides stand lovingly-
nursed *neepa* plantlets.

In the alcove above the marble gateway sits
the proud solemn statue of a lion.

Now hie home the pigeons of my love;
already the peacock is asleep on his golden
perch.

Now down the stairs walks my *Malabika*,
lamp in hand, pauses on the last step, a
goddess graceful as the evening star.

The fragrance of the saffron-powder on her
body and the incense of her hair envelop me
like a passionate sigh.

Through a gap in her loosening vestment
shows the design of sandal-paste painted on
her left breast.

And she stands like an image in the silence
of the evening, the hum of the city now
stilled.

At sight of me, my love slowly lowers the
lamp on the threshold and stands before me,
places her hand on mine and her sad eyes ask,
'In good cheer, my friend?'

My eyes on her, I try to reply but have no
words. We have forgotten the language we
once spoke, we have forgotten even our
names. We muse and muse but can remember
nothing. We gaze at each other and tears
stream down our eyes.

Under the gateway trees we stand pensive.
And then, I know not how her gentle hand
nestles within mine like a homing bird
yearning for its nest; her head gently lowers

itself on my breast like a drooping lotus; breath
mingles with breath in passionate silence.

Dark night obliterates the city of *Ujjain*, a
gust of wind puts out the lamp on the
threshold, and at the temple of Shiva on the
bank of the *Sipra*, the evening worship comes
to an end.

May, 1897
Swapna from 'Kalpana'

INVENTION OF SHOES

King Habu and Minister Gabu are the stock fools of Bengali folklore.

*S*aid King Habu, 'Listen, Minister Gabu.
All last night I pondered
Why my feet should catch the dust
Whenever they touch the earth.
All you officials here,
For your salaries you only care;
To State affairs you pay no heed,
And let my earth soil my feet.
What unearthly goings-on in my state!
But I warn you all:
This must be remedied at once, or heads will fall.'

The frightened Gabu into a cold sweat broke,
And nearly died of worry.
The pandits paled, the women wailed
And gave up cooking rice and curry.
All night long the courtiers try
In vain to wink an eye.
His tears down his grey beard streaming,
Gabu at the King's feet fell and said,
'How shall we kiss the dust of your feet
If your feet don't catch the dust?'

After thinking hard the King said, 'True.
But first things first
And last things last you should do.

First remove the dust,
Then solve the problem you have posed.
Why do I keep you all and so many
    Dee Es Cees,
If for lack of dust on the earth
You can't kiss the dust of my feet?'

So Gabu brought the learned and the wise,
Foreign and native, from far and near.
They fixed their glasses
On the tips of their noses,
And after a long session of thinking tough,
And using up nineteen barrels of snuff,
They said, 'If we carry out Your Majesty's
    desire,
The earth no longer any crops will bear.'
The King said, 'Then why are you here?'

After laying their heads again together,
Seventeen and a half lakhs of brooms they
    bought,
And gave every speck and spot
Of dust so great a clout,
And raised such a pother,
That the town was hid, the sun blotted out.
The dust blocked all noses, mouths and
    throats,
And of sneezing and coughing caused many a fit.
The King said, 'To rid the earth of dust
They fill it with it.'

Twenty-one lakhs of *bheesties** instantly ran
With skins slung on their backs;
Drained all rivers, lakes and ponds
Down to the mud,
And poured the water on land,
Causing a flood.
Creatures aquatic for lack of water died,
Those terrestrial the art of swimming tried.
Boats got stranded in mid-river,
The country was hit by colds and fever.
The King said, 'Lud,
The asses have turned the dust into mud.'

In conference the pandits sat again,
Of the problem of dust the solution to find;
They racked their brains, but in vain,
And nearly went out of their mind.
'Cover the earth with matting,' some said;
Some wanted it carpeted instead;
Some others advised the King to live in
     a room
Without a hole or a chink
In walls and roof,
And absolutely dust-proof.

The last advice the King found right.
But he was afraid his kingdom might
To ruin run,

---

* Water carriers.

If the dust to shun,
He shut himself in day and night.
So they advised him, all together,
To cover the earth with leather;
The dusty earth to pack
Within a leather sack;
And thus his name record
As the earth's sovereign lord.
The job, they said, would be done like a shot,
Once the right *chamar** he got.

Every one dropped the work on hand,
Sallied forth at once, and scoured the land.
Up and down they searched, in and around,
But the right *chamar*
Or the right leather nowhere found.
At last an old man,
Head of the *Chamar* clan,
His way very slowly made
To the King, and gently smiling said:
'I can show you, with your leave;
The easy way your object to achieve.
To cover the earth there is no need,
If you cover your own two feet.'

The King could not see
How a solution so easy
Would be at all commensurate

---

* Leather worker.

With a problem so obdurate.
'Imprison the rascal, impale him,'
The courtiers continued to blather,
While at the King's feet seated,
The old man cased them in leather.
'The idea is mine, my brain has been picked',
The Minister declared,
As shoes were invented,
And the earth was spared.

1897
Juta Abishkar from 'Kalpana'

SUMMER

Thou art the Great Destroyer, O *Vaisakh**
    stern and terrible.
Unkempt and dustladen stream thy brown
    matted locks,
weary with penance is thy parched body.
Whom dost thou summon with thy dread
    trumpet.
O Great Destroyer, O *Vaisakh* stern and
    terrible?

Thy insubstantial and shadowy followers—
they rush forth from crevices in the scorched
    coppery horizon.
In the silent and intense midday sky
thy shadowy and insubstantial followers
go wild with their fearful invisible dance.

The hot winds surge with wild energy.
They pirouette with burning breath in bursts
    of frenzied speed,
grass and leaves whirl in the mad dance,
crushed particles are churned in empty space
    in cyclonic rhythm
as the hot winds surge with wild energy.

---

* *Vaisakh*: 14th April–13th May, the hottest month in eastern India. Here the poet imagines
  Vaisakh as Shiva, the destroyer.

O emaciated ascetic with glowing eyes,
thou sittest with legs crossed in the lotus
    posture,
bloodshot eyeballs focussed on thy brow.
An alien wanderer in the bare fields by the
    waterless river bank,
O emaciated ascetic with glowing eyes.

Before thee burns a funeral pyre
that lifts its flaming tongue to lap the
    firmament.
The departed year, the world's discarded
    corpse,
burns to ashes in thy blazing fire.

O ascetic, sound now thy call of peace.
Let thy deep generous note spread to right
    and left,
Cross rivers, move from village to village,
    and fill the wide open spaces.
O ascetic, sound now thy call of peace.
With thy melancholy chant
let heart-breaking grief spread throughout
    the world:
Let it sound in the note of the weary dove,
in the tired murmur of the thin flow of
    the Ganges.
Let it merge with thy melancholy notes
    in the shadow of the peepul tree.

Let sorrow and joy, hope and despair
scatter in the sky like dust tossed by your
   breath.
Let sorrow and joy, hope and despair
fill up the expectant sky
with the fragrance of discarded flowers.

Spread O spread across the sky thy ochre
   ascetic robes.
Shield with thy great renunciation
old age and death, hunger and thirst,
millions of human hearts weary with thought.
Spread thy ochre robes across the sky.

Sound thy call, O *Vaisakh* stern and terrible.
My midday slumber rudely shattered
I shall come out into the open.
Speechless and still I shall gaze
at the horizon across burnt and lifeless fields:
O Great Destroyer, O *Vaisakh* stern and terrible.

1900
Vaisakh   from 'Kalpana'

THE LORD'S DEBT

*A*pace went news from village to village,
*Maitra Mahashay** was on pilgrimage bent to
where the Ganga merges into the sea. Quickly
enough there gathered around him company,
young and old. At the river ghat two country
boats lay ready.

'Let me come with you, *Thakur*',* prayed
Mokshada, a young widow, pining for piety.
Her eyes piteous and pleading, she would listen
to no reason and take no refusal. 'But there is
no room!' said Maitra, 'I cling to your feet',
she replied in tears, 'I will find room in some
corner.'

Won over by pity, the Brahmin asked still
in doubt: 'Haven't you a small child? Where
will he stay?'

'O, Rakhal?' the woman answered, 'he'll be
with his aunt, the one who brought him up. I
was long ill and Annada fed him and her own
child at her breast. Ever since, he prefers his
aunt to me and when he is naughty and I
punish him, why, his aunt takes his side and
hides him in her lap. He'll be happier, *Thakur*,
with her than with me.'

The Brahmin agreed and soon enough
Mokshada was ready. With her little packing

---

* '*Mahashay*' and '*Thakur*' are terms indicating respect.

done, she bowed at her elders' feet and took
sad leave of her friends.

At the ghat, who would she see but her
Rakhal? He had slipped from home early and
sat silent and unworried in the boat.

'You here?' his mother asked, and heard the
answer, 'Why, yes, I'm going to the sea.'

'You are, are you?' she shouted, 'come
down at once, you bandit-child!'

Again he said, his firm eyes wide open, 'I'm
going to the sea, mother!'

He clung to the boat's side as his mother
tried to drag him down. The Brahmin, moved
by pity, smiled and said 'Let be, let him stay.'

'All right', the mother suddenly blurted, 'I'll
leave you in the bottom of the sea!'

As she heard her own words, arrows of
remorse bit at her heart. *'Narayan! Narayan!'*
she muttered, invoking her god and took the
child in her arms, caressing him fondly.

In a quiet voice, Maitra whispered, 'What
madness possessed you that you spoke such evil
words?'

News travelled soon of Rakhal going with
the pilgrims. His aunt came rushing to the ghat
urging him to stay.

'I'll be back soon, auntie,' Rakhal smiled at
her, 'but I must really go to the sea!'

'My Rakhal is so naughty and I only can
manage him, and he's never been away from

me, *Thakur*' Annada pleaded. 'Don't take him, please; let me have him back.'

Rakhal would not bend and said, 'I tell you, auntie, I'll go now and come back soon.'

In affectionate tones the Brahmin said, 'Don't you fear for Rakhal! I shall be there and there's no worry. The winter days are here, the rivers and streams are calm, the roads are safe and crowds are going. Barely two months shall we need to go there and return. Your Rakhal will be safe with us.'

At the auspicious moment, invoking *Durga's** name, the boat moved off. On the ghat stood the village women, crying as they bade farewell. On the *Choorni's* bank the village looked tearful, bathed in *Hemanta's*† morning dew.

The fair over, the pilgrim groups started homeword. The old boat, tied again at the ghat, awaited the afternoon tide.

All wonder spent, Rakhal was famishing for home and his aunt's caress, his mind numbed by the ceaseless sight of unending waters. Waters that were dark and sleek and crooked and cruel, and like serpents lolled out hungry tongues. Wicked and deceitful waters that raised a million hoods and roared and moaned

---

* Durga: name of a goddess widely worshipped by Hindus.
† *Hemanta* : Late autumn.

79

everlastingly, mouth watering, as they yearned to devour Earth's children.

O Earth our loving mother, dumb but protective, you are hoary with age and tolerant of all truancies, our cradle of joy, softbosomed. How your unseen arms, O charming mother, draw us all the time, mightily, to your quiet, horizon-spanning heart!

The restive boy, his patience ended, asked again and again: 'When will flowtide come, *Thakur?*'

Animation suddenly shot through the tranquil waters. The river swelled, as if with tidings of hope. The boat turned right about, its ropes shivered and groaned. The triumphant sea marched up the river with the waves' thundering music. The tide had come and the boatmen, bowing before God, steered quickly northwards.

'When shall we reach home?' asked Rakhal, nestling up to the Brahmin.

Two leagues ahead, the sun not yet set, the north wind freshened. Sandbanks blocked Roopnarain's mouth and the river narrowed. There began tumult heady and strong, between the rowdy north wind and the oncoming tide.

The pilgrims cried aloud, 'Draw the boat ashore!' Ashore, but where was the shore?

All around were the frenzied waves tossing

in dread dance, beating time with a million hands, mocking the heavens in foam-speckled wrath. Far away showed the dim line of the distant forest. On all sides rose the greedy and angry waves like fierce proud rebels against the tranquil sunset.

The boat refused to obey the helm and span round and round like a restless foolish drunkard. The bitter wind mingled with the cold sweat of fear to make all tremble as on the day of doom.

Some had lost speech. Others shouted hoarsely or wept as they called on their kin. Face shrunken and pale, Maitra sat with eyes shut and muttered his prayers. Rakhal, in a cold tremor, hid his face in his mother's breast.

The boatman, desperate, suddenly called out, 'One in this boat has cheated the Lord, has offered Him a gift but has not kept his word. That explains this untimely storm and unruly waves. He must carry out his pledge. I warn you, you cannot flout an angry God!'

The pilgrims threw overboard whatever they had,—money and clothes and all, but to no avail. The waters again rushed fiercely on the boat.

'Listen before it is too late', the boatman cried again. 'Who is it is taking back what belongs to the God?'

Suddenly the Brahmin rose and pointed to

Mokshada, 'There's the woman who offered her child to God and is taking him back.'

Hearts merciless with fear, the pilgrims cried with one voice, throw him overboard.

'Save him, O save him', cried Mokshada, clasping Rakhal to her breast, 'Save him, *Thakur*, in the name of God save him.'

The Brahmin shouted back angrily, 'Am I his protector? You are his mother and yet in anger you offered him to God, and now I am to save him! You must pay God's debt and keep your vow or else all these people will drown.'

'I am a poor foolish woman', Mokshada wailed, 'Do you, my Lord, accept as truth what I said in sudden anger, you who are the Lord of the inmost heart? Did you not know how vain were my words? Did you only hear the word of my mouth but not of my heart?'

Even as she cried, the boatmen and the pilgrims tore Rakhal from her arms and threw him into the raging river. With set jaw and closed eyes, Maitra turned his face away, covering his ears with his hands.

'Aunt, O aunt' screamed Rakhal and suddenly Maitra felt lightning lash his heart. A hundred scorpions bit him as the helpless infant's last cry pierced into his ears like an arrow of fire.

'Hold! Hold!' the Brahmin shouted as his

eyes rested for a moment on Mokshada who had fainted at his feet.

For a second he saw the child's terror-stricken eyes as with a last piteous cry for its aunt it disappeared in the boiling waves. Two tiny fists desperately clutched at the sky and then were lost.

'I'll bring you back', cried the Brahmin, and plunged headlong into the river.

October, 1898
Devatar Grash from 'Katha'

A SOJOURN IN HELL

A VOICE

*W*here goest thou, King of kings?

SOMAKA

Who hails me? In this deep dark of the mist
region I can see naught. Hold your chariot
awhile, aerial messenger, let me look round.

A VOICE

Descend, pray descend, mighty Monarch,
journeying to the land of the gods.

SOMAKA

Who art thou? Whence dost thou speak?

A VOICE

I am Ritvik, once chief priest at your royal
court.

SOMAKA

Sire, all the tears of the universe, turned to
vapour, made this dread region of eternal
gloom. Sky untouched by sun or moon or stars,
massive sorrow weighs heavily with the
suffocation of an evil nightmare. Why art thou
here?

THE SHADES

Astride the pathway from Earth to Heaven lies
this region of sorrow called Hell. We, its
denizens, see above us the distant gleam of

84

Heaven's lights. We hear day and night the
swift chariot wheels of passing pilgrims to the
Land of Bliss, and sleep flies from our eyes as
they burn with envy. We see also, beneath us,
the green foliage of the Earth we left, we hear
the far murmur of its seven oceans.

RITVIK

Descend, Monarch, from thy chariot.

THE SHADES

Listen to the prayers of the creatures of misery
and stay with us a brief hour. The compassions
of the Earth fill thy heart still. Thou barest in
thy spirit the fragrance of grass and leaf and
flower and the inner offerings from friend and
brother and woman. Thou barest the diverse
joy of the Earth's changing seasons.

SOMAKA

Sire, why hast thou been doomed to live in
this dark realm?

RITVIK

I cast thy son into the sacrificial fire. I must
expiate for that crime.

THE SHADES

Tell us the story, O King, of what happened
on the earth. Accounts of evil deeds still stir us
with wistful excitement. Thou hast in thy
voice the tones of earthly music, the tremors of

joy and pain. Let us have the story in that human voice.

SOMAKA

Listen, then, O Shades. I am Somaka, ruler of the kingdom of Videha. Without offspring for long years, I had a son at last in my old age, the fruit of many prayers to the gods and sages and Brahmins. The bonds of my new love held me in complete thrall and I forgot all else. He, my son, was the divine nectar in my thirst-ridden life. He, like a solitary white blossom, covered the stem of my being. My heart shone upon face, like the sun upon earth. I guarded him with the alarmed care of a lotus leaf holding a dewdrop. The king and warrior in me frowned upon the fond parent. The kingdom felt shamed at my neglect of the royal duties and obligations.

One day, at the court, while deep in work with my counsellors, I heard the sharp wail of my child. Instantly I stepped down from my throne and rushed off to the inner apartments.

RITVIK

At that self-same moment I, chief priest of the kingdom, entered the court to give the Ruler my blessings and sacrificial gifts. In his haste he pushed me aside scattering the gifts and rushed along. The Brahmin's pride in me, affronted and hurt, flared up. Soon the king returned

86

and sat shamefacedly on his throne. I
addressed him then:

'What sudden catastrophe had befallen, O
King, that you had to rush away, heedless of a
Brahmin's hand lifted to offer benediction?
What forced you to quit your royal duties?
There were the men waiting with petitions to
secure justice; there were envoys from many
kingdoms and your own feudal chiefs waiting
to be received; there were the high officials
who needed directives on matters of State. At
that busiest of all hours you happened to hear
a child cry and quit all, speeding crazily to the
inner chambers. Fie, Monarch! The warriors at
court sit with heads bowed in shame because
of the weakness of their master. Our enemies
in lands far and near laugh to see a king
enchained, helpless, in the arms of an infant.
And our friends, embarrassed and unhappy,
wipe the mist in their eyes in secret.'

SOMAKA

Words of such sharp reproach dazed the court.
My counsellors and subjects and the dignitaries
and visitors from far kingdoms were struck
silent and looked at me in wondering alarm.
For a moment I felt the swift surge of
resentment, and then shame smote down the
roused serpent of wrath. I bowed my head to
the feet of the priest and humbly said,

'Sire, one child is all that I have. I am ever

87

troubled by concern on his account.
Overcome by my feeling I have acted wrongly.
I beg of you to pardon me. Listen, my
counsellors; listen, friends from other lands.
Never again shall I be guilty of such
transgression; never shall I do a thing that
would dim the bright heritage of the *kshatriya*
race.'

RITVIK

The court sat hushed, but happy. I alone
spoke. I spoke with the heat of wounded
conceit still burning in me.

'Wouldst thou be freed from the curse of
having one son alone? There is a way. But it is
a hard way. I doubt if you can take it'.

The King answered firmly:

'There is naught on earth that the son of
Kshatriya, the brave warrior caste, cannot do.
Touching thy feet I take an irrevocable
pledge.'

I smiled and lifted my voice: 'Listen, then,
O Monarch. I shall make preparations to light
a great sacrificial fire. Thou shalt make a
votive offering to the fire. Thou shalt offer it
thine infant son. The queens, filling their
breath with the consecrated smoke from the
consumed body of the child, shall conceive
and bear a hundred sons. That is my
injunction.'

The King hung his head, speechless, while the royal court burst into a loud chorus of rage: 'Fie, Brahmin. Fie for the sinful and brutal proposal.'

The Ruler lifted his voice at last and his voice was calm:

'Sire, be it so. The pledge of a *kshatriya* shall be fulfilled.'

The wails of women echoed in the palace. Cries of horror-struck protest rang in the city streets. The royal troops were poised for revolt. Yet the King stood his ground. He was immovable as a rock.

The sacrificial fire was lit. But there was not a soul, and not a single hand that would fetch the infant prince from the inner chambers. Servants refused to obey the order. Courtiers stood by in sullen silence. The guards wiped tears. Soldiers flung their arms aside and walked away.

I, chief priest of the kingdom, versed in sacred lore and free from the ties of delusion, firm in my belief that the bonds of affection were nothing but vanity, strode into the inner apartments. The queens crowded with anxious fear around the child and shielded him with their bodies, even as a hundred branches hold a rare flower in protection. At sight of me the child lifted his arms and laughed. In half-formed child language he seemed to say: 'Take me away. Pierce the walls of my prison; let me be free awhile'. For he was cramped and bored, needing escape.

I answered his unspoken wish with a friendly laugh: 'Come with me. Let me cut the chains of affection that hold you helplessly bound. I shall give you freedom.'

I swept the women aside and snatched the smiling child away from his mother's arms and from all the arms raised protectively. The baffled women fell at my feet, clasping them prayerfully, barring my way, but I freed myself and rushed off.

The sacrificial fire was ablaze and beside it stood the King, carven cut of stone. The child, smiling and happy reached out toward the inviting wonder of the flames.

A hundred-throated lamentation from the palace lifted skyward. On the streets the Brahmins cursed me aloud and walked away from the city, overshadowed, as they said, by an unspeakable crime. But I, tranquil as ever, spoke:

'O Monarch, hold thy child in thine arms and offer him to the Fire-god while I chant the sacred words of *mantra*.'

SOMAKA

Stop! Speak no more of that evil hour.

THE SHADES

Stop, for shame! We in our earth-lives were
guilty of many a heinous deed, but you, Ritvik,
far surpass us all and deserve a Hell all to
yourself, built for you alone. There is no sinner
here foul enough for your company.

AERIAL MESSENGER

King, why dost thou pause in this Hell, sharing
the torments of the sinners? Ascend the
chariot and let us be off. Do not re-live the
painful past.

SOMAKA

Take back thy chariot, messenger of the gods. I
will not proceed to Heaven. My place is here
with that ill-fated Brahmin. Drunk with my
Kshatriya pride, seeking to hide my failure to
do my duty, I, a father, gave my innocent child
to the flames. To proclaim the strength of my
warrior spirit and confound my denouncers, I
assigned to the flames my humanity, my royal
duty and my fatherly heart. The flames have
consumed me since, every day, every hour,
until the moment of my death. Even now,
though released from earthly life I feel the
burning deep in my accursed soul. My son, all
innocence and tenderness, loving and feeding
on love, hailed the bright fire as a gift from his
fond father and trustfully held out his arms.
Then suddenly, under the flames, what pained

91

surprise, what rebuke, filled his agonised face!

No, Hell's conflagration cannot exceed the burning in my heart. I, assigned a place in Heaven? The gods might have overlooked my crime, but can I ever forget that last pained glance of my child at the touch of fire, his hurt accusation? Day and night, without cease, I shall let myself be tormented in Hell, yet it would be scant retribution.

(*Enter, Dharma, the god of Right Conduct*)

DHARMA

Heaven awaits thee, O King. Do not tarry any longer.

SOMAKA

That is no place, O God, for one who has destroyed his own child.

DHARMA

You have known hell on earth itself. That was your atonement. Your sin has been burnt out in the fires of agony lit in your soul. This Hell is fit abode for the Brahmin who, in the pride of his false wisdom, snatched a child from its nest of love and destroyed it and knew no remorse.

RITVIK

Do not go away, pray. Stay back, O King of kings. Let not the agony of envy be added to my other torments. For, departing alone to

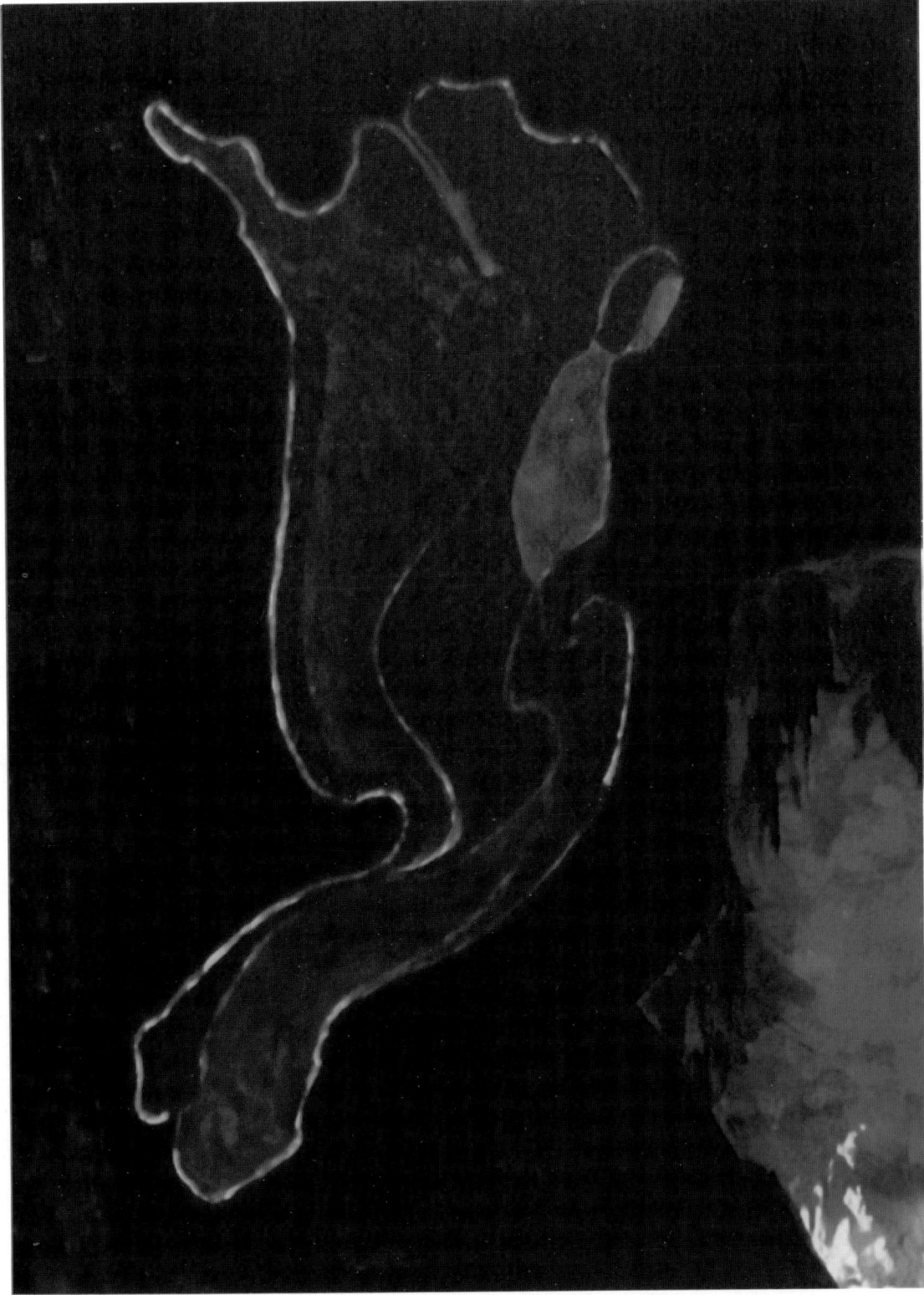

Heaven, thou shalt create a second Hell for
me, twice unbearable.

SOMAKA

I shall stay with thee, ill-fated one. You and I
together shall make our votive *homa* offerings
to the massive flames of Hell. O Dharma, grant
me this wish. Let me stay in hell with Ritvik
until his redemption.

DHARMA

Be it so. Stay here in the glory of thy spirit.
Let the light on thy brow shield thee from the
unbearable. Let hell-fire be thy proud throne
of gold.

THE SHADES

King of kings, who has relinquished the fruits
of virtue! Sinless denizen of Hell! Let the
power of thy great sacrifice kindle a spark in
the hearts of the sinners who will have thy
company. Let Hell itself be redeemed and
touched by salvation. Give thy hand to thine
arch-enemy, as though he were your dearest
friend, and share with him the age-long
wretchedness. Atop the fiery peak of nameless
misery, even as sunshine on a bitter cloud,
your twin images shall be set, visible for all
time—lustrous honour and dark ignominy.

November, 1898
Narak Bash from 'Kahini'

KARNA AND KUNTI

KARNA. Engaged in worship of the evening Sun
on the banks of the sacred Ganga, I am he
who is called Karna, son of Adhiratha, the
charioteer, born of Radha.

Now tell me Lady who are you?

KUNTI. My child, on the first morning of your
life I introduced you to this world. Today I
have shed all sense of shame and come to
reveal myself to you.

KARNA. Lady, the glance of your lowered eyes
melts my heart,—as melts the ice when
sunlight strikes the mountain peak. Your voice
comes from across a previous birth, and evokes
a strange pain as it greets my ears.

Tell me O Lady unknown, what bond of
mystery links my birth with you?

KUNTI. My child, be patient for a while. Let
first my Lord the Sun go down. Let evening
darkness gather.

Now I can tell you who I am, I am Kunti.

KARNA. You are Kunti the mother of Arjuna?

KUNTI. Yes, I am the mother of Arjuna, but do
not nurse in your heart, my child, hate for me
on that account. I remember even today when
in Hastinapur, there was a trial of arms. You
slowly came upon the stage, a youthful figure
like the new-born Sun in the star-studded

94

eastern sky. Of all the women who sat behind the screen, wretched who was she that could not speak and yet felt in her riven heart the pangs of unsatisfied affection like the sting of a thousand serpents? Who was she whose eyes kissed every limb of yours in silent benediction?

It was me, the mother of Arjuna.

When Kripa came and asked your father's name and said that none could fight Arjuna unless he was born of Kings, you blushed with shame; you spoke no words, and stood silent with lowered face. Hopeless who was she that felt the blush of shame upon your face like a scaring flame in her heart?

It was me, Arjuna's mother.

All honour to son Duryodhana, who forthwith crowned you king. God bless him for his act. Tears welled out of my eyes, and sought to drop upon your head like consecrated waters of coronation.

Suddenly I saw the charioteer Adhiratha press his way into the court in speechless joy. You hailed the old charioteer, saluted him as your father, and placed your new crowned head upon his feet in the midst of a crowd of curious courtiers. The friends of the Pandavas smiled in derison, but at that moment, who hailed you in proud affection as a hero among heroes?

It was me, the mother of Arjuna.

KARNA. My salutations honoured lady. You, the Queen mother, why are you here alone? This is the battlefield and I am the General of the Kauravas.

KUNTI. My son, I have come to ask you a favour. Do not send me back disappointed.

KARNA. A favour from me! I promise that I shall place at your feet whatever you may want except my manhood and my faith.

KUNTI. I have come to take you back.

KARNA. Where will you take me?

KUNTI. To my famished heart, to your mother's arms.

KARNA. You are, my lady, Fortune's favourite, and blessed with five heroes as your sons. I am a minor king without pride of wealth or lineage. Where will you find a place for me?

KUNTI. I shall place you on the highest seat, I shall place you before all my other sons. You are my eldest born.

KARNA. By what right shall I enter into the kingdom of your love? Your sons have been denied their realm. Tell me by what right shall I deprive them of the fullness of their mother's love?

A mother's love cannot be bought by the turn of dice, prowess cannot win a mother's heart. It can come only as a gift of God.

96

KUNTI. My son, you once came to me with God-given claim. Come back today to your birthright in honour and glory. Come without any hesitation. Come and take your place in your mother's arms along with your brothers.

KARNA. My lady, I hear your voice like a dream from afar. Look, the darkness covers all around. The world is swept away. Even the Ganges flows without a sound. You have taken me to a magic world, to a forgotten home in the very dawn of awakening.

Your message touches my heart like an old eternal truth. It seems to me that my budding childhood—like the darkness in the mother's womb—surrounds me once again. I do not know whether it is the truth or a dream. But come O Queen mother, come to me as image of my mother's love. Keep for a moment your right hand on my brow. For a moment touch my face. I have often heard men say my mother abandoned me. Often I have dreamt at night that my lost mother came with slow sad steps to look at me. With anguished heart I have wept, 'O mother dear take off your veil and let me look at you.' In a flash the image vanished and rent my hungry eager dreams. Is it my fate that here this night on this battlefield on Ganga's shore, that dream will take form as the mother of the Pandavas?

Look, Lady, in the distant bank the lights shine in the camp of the Pandavas. On this

97

bank not far away you can hear the thousand stallions stamping their heels in the stables of the Kauravas. Tomorrow morning the decisive battle will begin. Why did I hear tonight in the voice of Arjuna's mother my mother's loving tone? Why did my name ring such music in her voice? My heart yearns towards the five Pandavas and seeks to greet them as brothers dear.

KUNTI. Come with me my child—then come with me.

KARNA. I will come with you, mother mine. I will come and ask no questions. I will permit no doubts. I will have no thought trouble my soul. My lady, you are my mother. My inmost soul awakens to your call. I can no longer hear the drum of war nor the conch of victory. Conflict born of hatred, hero's fame and even victory and defeat all seem alien now. Take me where you will.

KUNTI. I shall take you to the other side where burns the lamp in the silent tent on the pale sandy river bank.

KARNA. The orphan child will find there his mother lost. The Pole-star will throughout the night shine in splendid beauty in your eyes. My lady, tell me once again I am your son.

KUNTI. You are my son.

KARNA. Why then did you cast me far away in

indignity into a strange blind world—a child
without lineage, respect or mother's love?
Why did you let me float away for good in the
currents of cold contempt? Why did you
banish me from the company of my brothers
all these days? You kept Arjuna and me apart
and from our childhood, a deep invisible pull
has drawn us with the resistless bond of hate.

You are silent, my mother? It seems your
shame burns through the darkness of the
night, touches all my limbs in mute silence,
makes me close my eyes.

Be it so, mother mine. You need not say why
you abandoned me. God's first gift to man in this
cruel world is a mother's love. You need not tell
me now why you robbed your own child of his
birth-right and the gift of God. I would only like
to know why have you come to call me back
today?

KUNTI. My child, your words pierce through my
heart like a hundred thunderbolts and shatter
it to fragments.

I cast you away—that curse has always
made me feel childless even when five sons
clung to me. My arms sought you throughout
the world and I longed to draw you near. The
son whom I denied is the one for whom my
heart has lit the flaming lamp.

Through long life I burnt myself in the
worship of the Lord of the world in seeking

my rejected son. Today at last I am fortunate, for I have found you again. When your lips could not speak a word, I did you grievous wrong my child. With the same lips, forgive me today. Your forgiveness will be more powerful than bitter condemnation, will light a fire that will burn my sins away and make me pure again.

KARNA. Give me the dust of your feet, my mother. In return, take my tears.

KUNTI. My son, I have not come to you in the hope that I shall take you to my heart and find new happiness. I have come to bring you to your rightful place. You are not the son of a charioteer, you are the son of kings. Cast behind all humiliation, come and take your place with your five brothers.

KARNA. Lady, I am the son of a charioteer. My mother is Radha. I do not know of any honour greater than this. Let the Pandavas remain Pandavas. Let the Kauravas remain Kauravas. I feel no jealousy for either of them.

KUNTI. My child, you must recover your throne by the might of your arms. Yudhishtra will fan you with the white fan. Bhima will hold the umbrella over your head. Arjuna will be your charioteer. The priest Dhaumya will chant the Vedic hymns. Conqueror of all enemies, you will remain unrivalled on your jewelled throne in the splendour of your power among your friends.

KARNA. A throne? You are offering the promise of a realm to one who has rejected the claims of a mother's love? The wealth of which you deprived me at my birth is today beyond your power to give.

At the moment of my birth at one stroke you denied me, mother dear, my mother, my brothers and my kingly line.

If today I deny the carter's wife and hail as my mother the Royal Queen, if today I sunder the bonds which tie me to the king of Kauravas and seek to find myself a throne, shame be on me.

KUNTI. You are a hero my son, you are blessed. How stern and relentless Your judgement, Lord. Who knew that day when I cast a helpless child that he would grow in strength and might and return from dark oblivion to strike with cruel hands the children of his own mother's womb? What a curse is this?

KARNA. Have no fear, mother mine. I tell you that the Pandavas will win. Tonight I have read on this dark table of the night by the dim light of stars the dismal result of this war.

In this calm silent moment, there comes into my mind from the eternal sky the music of endeavour that must fail, the energy of action

101

that has no hope. I can see with calm detachment the emptiness of the final result.

Do not ask me mother to desert the side that is doomed to defeat. Let the Pandavas be victorious. Let them be kings. I shall remain among those who failed, those whose life was fruitless.

At the moment of my birth you flung me to the dust, nameless and homeless. Leave me again tonight with stern heart among the unnamed, the unknown and the defeated. Only this benediction leave for me. Neither the lure of victory nor of fame nor of realm may ever turn me from the path of rectitude.

March, 1900
Karna Kunti Sambad from 'Kahini'

102

THE RIGHT PLACE

*W*here, in which market, would you be on
sale, my song? Where would you choose your
niche?

Would you care for the cloister of the
pedants who take snuff and scatter the powder
all around while they chop logic to determine
whether Cause is in Effect or Effect is in
Cause; where MSS and *editio princeps* cure you
of errors?

There in a corner would you have a seat?

Listening, my song murmurs, 'No, no,
certainly not!'

Where, in which market, would you be on
sale, my song? Which way can allure you?

Yonder in his palace lives the man of
fortune. Five thousand books decorate his
mahogany shelves. No one turns over the
leaves, the golden inscriptions are untouched;
like unsmelt jasmines they stand; it is only the
servants who daily dust them with care.

Is that the place, my song, you would go to?

Listening, my song whispers, 'No, no,
certainly not!'

Where, in which market, would you be on
sale, my song? Where is the honour you covet?

There's a place where the youthful
examinee pores on cribs while his attention
strays. Before him are open unreadable texts
while books of verse are hid for fear of
disapproving elders.

There in that room all is untidy, topsy-
turvy, will you play there, my restless song, will
you?

Listening, my song wavers, to go or not to go!

Where, in which market, would you be on
sale, my song? Where would you feel free?

There where the young housewife works in
her pantry but flies to her bedroom when she
has a moment to spare and pulls out a book of
verses hidden under a pillow, its pages
damaged by a turbulent child.

Would you go there where her undone bed
is smeared with vermilion tint and mascara
smudge?

Listening, my song holds her breath,
tremulous with longing.

Where, in which market, would you be on
sale, my song? Where will you be vitalised?

Is it the place where a love-enraptured

couple wander about looking for a shady
secluded nook, where birds sing them songs, a
river chants ballads, and flowers and leaves
and creepers articulate a hundred cadences.

There close by frank laughter and tear-
glistened eye-lashes, in the midst of the
orchestral music of the universe, will you, my
song, be?

'There, there indeed is my niche!' Suddenly
exclaims my song.

1900
Jathasthan from 'Kshanika'

IMMODESTY

*M*y incomparable One,
Forgive me if per chance I am indiscreet today.
It is the first day of *Asadh*:
The woodlands are languid with yearning,
The *bakul* avenue is dizzy with buds
And the newly-blossomed *kadamba* intoxicates
    with its fragrance.

My incomparable One,
Forgive me if my stare offends you today.
See yonder, from one end of the sky to another
The lightning flashes incessantly,
In quick curiosity peeps through your
    casement,
And the wind rushes into your room to play a
    boisterous game.

My incomparable One,
Forgive me if a numbness touches my song today.
Rain pours down tumultuously,
Babbling waves break on the river-banks
Young leaves rustle and murmur through
    the woods,
And the moist wind spreads its cloudy ballads
    in all corners of the earth.

My incomparable One,
Forgive me if my manners are at fault today.
In this dimly-lit universe,
No one need be occupied with work;
Roads and meadows are lonely and still as a
    painting
And the world is shrouded in cold cloud-heavy
    darkness.

My incomparable One,
Forgive me if per chance I am indiscreet today.
On your dark eyes
Descends the shadow of dark *Asadh.*
A garland of white jasmine circles your dark
    black curls
And your brow is the altar of the young
    rainy season.

June, 1900
Abinay from 'Kshanika'

কৃষ্ণকলি

কৃষ্ণকলি আমি তারেই বলি,
    কালো তারে বলে গাঁয়ের লোক —
মেঘলা দিনে দেখেছিলেম মাঠে
    কালো মেয়ের কালো হরিণ-চোখ!
মাথার 'পরে ছিল না তার বাস,
    মুক্ত বেণী পিঠের 'পরে লোটে;
কালো? তা সে যতই কালো হোক,
    দেখেছি তার কালো হরিণ-চোখ!

ঘন মেঘে আঁধার হল দেখে
    ডাকতে এল শ্যামল দুটি গাই,
শ্যামা মেয়ে ব্যস্ত ব্যাকুল পায়ে
    কুটীর হতে বাহির হল তাই !
আকাশপানে হানি যুগল ভুরু

KRISHNAKALI

In the village they call her the dark girl,
but to me she is the flower Krishnakali.
On a cloudy day in a field
I saw the dark girl's dark gazelle-eyes.
She had no covering on her head,
her loose hair had fallen on her back.

    Dark? However dark she be,
    I have seen her dark gazelle-eyes.

Two black cows were lowing,
as it grew dark under the heavy clouds.
So with anxious, hurried steps,
the dark girl came from her hut.
Raising her eyebrows toward the sky,
she listened a moment to the clouds' rumble.

    Dark? However dark she be,
    I have seen her dark gazelle-eyes.

A gust of the east wind
rippled the rice plants.
I was standing by a ridge,
alone in the field.
Whether or not she looked at me
Is known only to us two.

Dark? However dark she be,
I have seen her dark gazelle-eyes.

This is how the Kohl-dark cloud
rises in the north-east in *Jaistha;**
the soft dark shadow
descends on the *tamal* † grove in *Asharha;**
and sudden delight floods the heart
in the night of *Sravana.**

Dark? However dark she be,
I have seen her dark gazelle-eyes.

To me she is the flower Krishnakali,
whatever she be called by others.
In a field in Maynapara village
I saw the dark girl's dark gazelle-eyes.
She did not cover her head,
not having the time to feel embarrassed.

Dark? However dark she be,
I have seen her dark gazelle-eyes.

June, 1900
Krishnakali from 'Kshanika'

---

* Three months from midsummer to the end of the rainy season, and roughly corresponding
to June, July and August.
† A tree.

FALSE ALARM

*A*las, beloved! Is this the way to react to my
parting words? A smile flickers in the corner of
your eyes. So often have I said I am going and
then stayed on that you seem to think this
man will never go. He will hang on near the
door and come back.

If you ask me I shall tell you the truth; I also
think I shall come back. Spring days do come
back, the full moon smiles again, *Bakuls* bloom
anew on bare branches,—none of them
departs for ever. They go away a thousand
times and come back.

But, please, let a little doubt yet linger in your
mind. Give not a straight answer to the lie.
Shed a few mistaken tears, even though for a
moment, when in a choked voice I tell you
that I am leaving. You can laugh if you want
to when I come back.

1900
Viday Reet from 'Kshanika'

111

VITALITY

The vitality that flows in waves night and
day through every vein of my body, flows out
to conquer the universe; pulsates through the
world in amazing rhythm and cadence; inspires
every pore of the earth's soil with the thrill of
a million grass-blades growing; blossoms into
flowers and young leaves; sways, year after year,
in the ceaseless ebb and flow of the undulating
world-wide sea of life and death.

That endless vitality, absorbed into my
being, exalts me in every limb.

In my veins dances today that vast rhythm
of aeons.

1901
E amar sharirer shirae shirae . . .
from 'Naivedya'

DELIVERANCE

*S*alvation in a hermit's cave?
  No, not for me.

I shall retain a thousand ties and in their
midst savour the bliss of liberation.
I shall take this world, this jar of clay, and
fill it again and again with your nectar that has
many flavours and colours.
I shall light the lamp of my universe, and
with its million wicks illumine your temple.

I shall not shut the doors of my senses—no,
never. The joy of song, and sight, and
fragrance,—I shall keep them all and through
them gain the joy of meeting you.

Then shall my craving burn itself out in
freedom and my love find its fulfilment in
devotion.

1901
Bairagya sadhame mukti se amar noy . . .
from 'Naivedya'

113

THE STAFF OF JUSTICE

O King of kings, you have shared with every
man the burden of your justice, in each hand
You have placed a royal sceptre.

    Bless me that I may accept with humility
this exalted privilege.
    Give me strength to perform the harsh
duties of my station, revering You and fearing
none on earth.

    Where to forgive is to be cowardly, there,
O Punisher, let me ever be ruthless in Your
service. At a sign from You, let my speech
become a flaming sword of truth.
    In Your hall of justice, let me find my
proper place and fill it worthily.

    The unjust tyrant and he who meekly
bears—may both be consumed like heaps of
straw in the blazing fire of Your holy wrath.

1901
Tomar nayer dandya . . .
from 'Naivedya'

114

ALONE

*S*leep thou tonight. I shall sit watching by thy door and keep the light burning.

So long thou didst love, from now on I shall have to love thee in loneliness.

Thou will never again adorn thyself for my sake, but I shall through long days and nights deck my heart with flowers for thee.

Oblivious of fatigue and pain, thy arms have till now served me tirelessly but today I shall relieve them of all work and place them on my brow.

Thou hast offered thy mind and body and today thy worship done, thou departest from me, but from today my homage of tears and hymns of adoration shall be for thee alone.

January, 1903
Ajike tumi ghumao ami jagi rabo duare . . .
from 'Smaran'

115

THE WISE ONE

*Y*our little girl understands nothing, mother,
  your little girl is altogether a baby.
When we were flying a balloon,
  she thought a star was up in the sky!
When I am at a make-believe game of feast,
  and heap pebbles on a plate,
She thinks it is all real food
  and stuffs a handful into her mouth!
If I open a Child's Primer before her
  and say, 'Baby, now begin your study,'
She starts tearing off the pages;
  What kind of study is this, tell me!
If I cover my head with a piece of cloth
  and crawl towards her slowly,
You little girl bursts into tears,
  she thinks it is a voodoo witch!
If ever I am moved to anger,
  and scold her with glaring eyes,
Your little girl bursts into tinkling laughter.
  Does she think it's just a game?
Everyone knows that daddy has gone abroad,
  but if I were only to say, 'There comes
  daddy,'
She starts looking in all directions,
  so naive and simple is your baby!
When the laundryman comes to our house,
  I begin to instruct his young ass;

116

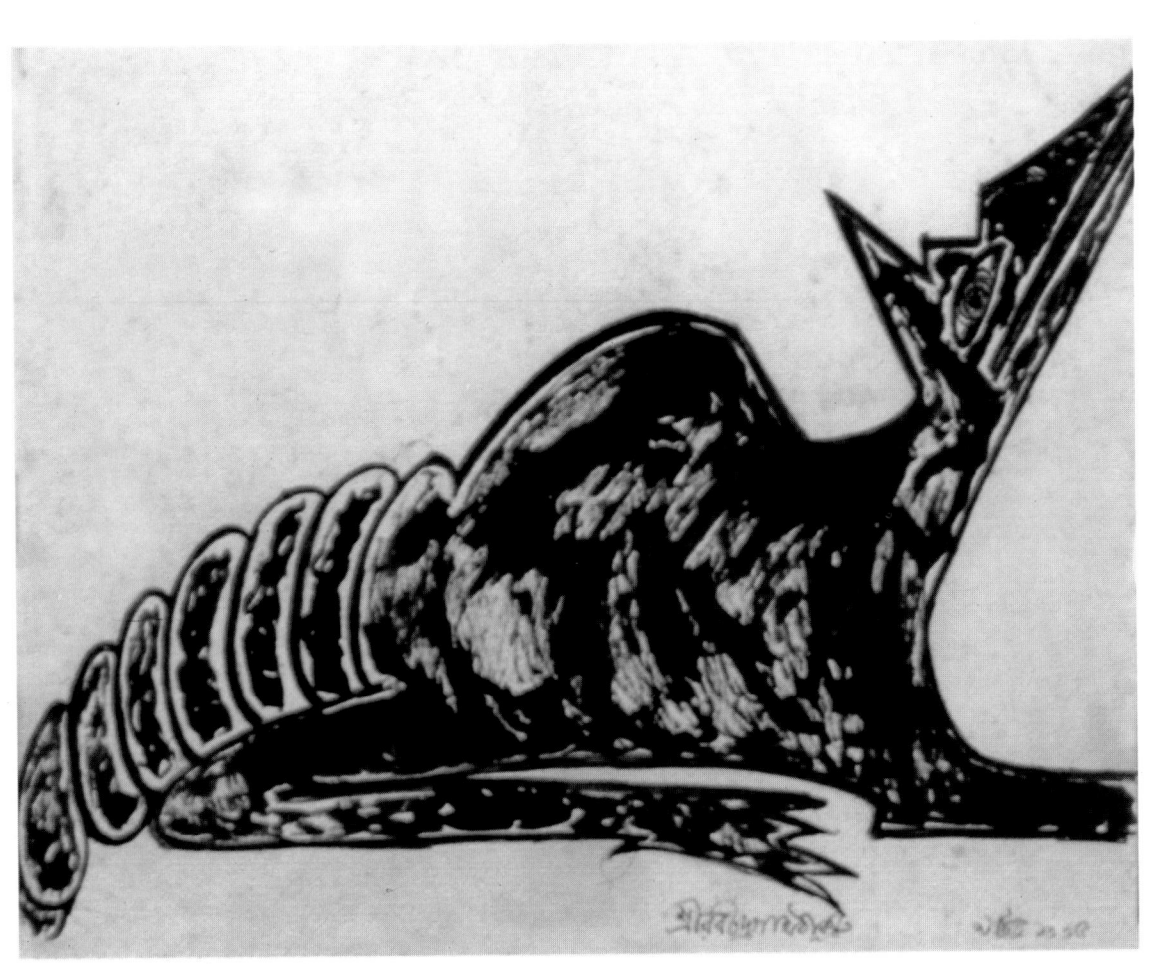

I say, 'Look, I am your teacher,'
    But baby addresses me as 'Brother', not 'Sir'
    in correct form.
She wishes to catch hold of the moon,
    She mumbles the name of Ganesh as Ganush!
Your little girl understands nothing, mother,
    Your little girl is altogether a baby.

1904
Bigya *from 'Shishu'*

THE CRITIC

*D*addy writes books, mother, does he? Books that none can understand? He read out to you the other day. Tell me, mother, what you made of that.

What is the good indeed of writing such books?

You tell me lovely stories, why doesn't he write such too? Didn't my granny tell him tales of adventures and princes?

Or has he perhaps forgotten all those stories!

When it's late for bathing time, you remind him again and again. It's time for dinner, you wait for him, but he hardly remembers such things.

All day long he plays at the writing game.

If while playing I go to Dad's room, 'Naughty boy', you call me. You scold me if I shout, 'Dad's busy writing, don't you see?'

Now tell me, mother, tell me, what's the use of writing?

When I pull out Dad's writing book and fetch pen and ink to write, and I write a b c x y z, why are you so cross with me?

You never say a word when Daddy does the
writing.

Doesn't he spoil sheets and sheets of ruled
paper? If I wish to make a paperboat, you say
paper mustn't be spoilt.

Is it a good thing, mother, to cover paper
with black marks?

1903
Samalochak from 'Shishu'

মনে কর যেন বিদেশ ঘুরে

মাকে দিয়ে পালিয়ে আবার দূরে।

তুমি যাচ্ছ পালকীতে মা চড়ে

দয়া করে একটুকু ফাঁক করে,

আমি যাচ্ছি তোমার পাশে,

চিনবামিনে তোমায়।

রাস্তা দিয়ে তোমার সুরে সুরে

রাঙর বুলের

মস্ত হল সূর্য নামে পাটে

এলেম যেন জোড়াদিঘির মাঠে।

দুপুর করে যে দিকপালের চাই

কোনোখানে জনমানব নাই,

তুমি যেন মনের মাঝে তাই

ভয় পেয়েছ ভারি এমন কোথা।

আমি বলছি ভয় কোরোনা মাগো

ঐ দেখা যায় মরা নদীর চোরা।

THE HERO

*I*magine, mother, I am taking you
to far-off foreign lands:
You in a palankeen with doors ajar,
and I beside on a chestnut horse,
its hoofs clop-clopping,
and raising little clouds of reddish dust.

At sundown hour we come one day
to a dying river's trickling stream,
and two large ponds, alike and close together,*
in a bare waste land
that stretches on and on
without a sign of man.
I see you are worried about where we have come,
and I say 'Mother, have no fear.'

If any cattle were there by day,
at nightfall back to the village have gone.
A track we strike that twists and turns
through the weeds and thorns that cover that land.
We grope our way in the dark, until
'What's that light by the ponds?' you say.

And all at once, 'Yo-ho-ho-ho'
aloud they shout, and fast they come.
Seized with fear, the trembling bearers

---

* Pairs of ponds were quite common in Bengal. Such a watering place would be a good haunt of bandits in folk-lore.

121

drop the palankeen, and cower on the thorns.
To God you pray, but calmly I say
'Have no fear, I am here.'

With clubs in their hands, china roses
stuck on their ears,* the mop-heads come.
I give them warning: 'Stop where you are,
and take a good look at this my sword.
If you come but one step nearer,
to bits and pieces I'll cut you up.'
And up they leap, their clubs they shake,
aloud they 'yo-ho-ho-ho'.

'Don't go near them, my son,' you cry.
'Just be quiet and see,' I say,
and riding fast I charge those men.
The fight that follows, the arms that clash,
the heads that fall, the men who flee
will make you shiver but to hear.

Just when you're thinking I've been killed,
fighting so many men alone,
I come back, soaked in sweat and blood,
and say the fight is over and won.
Out of the palankeen you joyfully come,
you take me in your arms, and give me a kiss,
and say how terrible it would have been
if you didn't have your boy with you.

---

* In Bengali folk-lore bandits wear *java* (hibiscus or China roses) flowers on their ears.

The things that happen day by day,
how I wish they were true like this!
My fight with the bandits would then be a tale
to make all hearers dumb with wonder.
Only big brother would doubt its truth,
would doubt if a little boy was so strong.
But all our neighbours would say you were lucky
to have had me with you, mother, that day.

1903
Bir Purush from 'Shishu'

RESTLESS

I am restless. I am athirst for Afar.

Time moves by; absent minded I sit and wait—wistful for Afar.

A longing deep within thirsts for thy distant touch.

O Great Beyond, with thy flute call intense passionate, thou makest me forget I am rooted, wingless.

I am eager and wakeful, I am a stranger in a strange land.

Thy breath comes to me whispering an impossible hope. Thy tongue is known to my heart as its very own.

O Far-to-seek, with thy flute call intense, passionate, thou makest me forget I know not the way and have no winged horse.

The mind soars off towards Afar and leaves me listless.

In the laze of a sun drenched noon, in the murmur of trees and the play of light and shade what an image fills my vision,—the image of Afar.

O Farthest End, with thy flute call intense, passionate, thou makest me forget the locked door of my prison cell.

1903
Ami chanchala he ami sudurer piyashi . . . from 'Utsarga'

THE ETERNAL CYCLE

*F*rankincense, flame-tipped, seeks to fade
    away in scent,
Scent seeks to house itself in frankincense.
The tune wants to be trapped into rhyme,
Rhyme wants to dissolve into tune.
The Idea needs embodiment in image,
Image its airy release into thought.
The infinite longs for communion with the
    finite,
The finite longs to be lost in the infinite.
From creation to demolition and back,
Such is the strange chain of ceaseless interflow;
The captive ever seeks to be free,
The free longs for the bondage of abode.

1903
Dhup apanare milaite chahe gandhe . . .
from 'Utsarga'

BIRTH AND DEATH

*I*t was only the other day that I come into this world, speechless, like a stranger without an introduction, poor, empty-handed, my cry my only wherewithal.

Yet today, the love of man draws from me all my songs. Lord of the Universe, Thou takest but little space in my heart, for Thou hast filled all of it with the world. The offering of new songs in new measures that I make everyday at Thy feet—that, too, others take when my worship is done, giving me their love as Thou hast given.

Ever do I cherish the hope that wherever Thou mayst lead me, in strange lands, Thou shalt bind me in bonds of love like this.

In the light of that love shall I unfold ever new petals to blossom forth in worlds beyond worlds. All the honey stored in the core of my heart will flow out in undiminishing tenderness drawn by the power of love.

In life after life in Thy vast
universe shall I follow the call of
Thy love, and leave behind me the
fragrance of endless lives and the
changing hues of ceaseless
unfoldment.

Who wants to live unchanged in
the same unchanging world, sunk in
the dark and narrow well of Eternity?
Rather shall I through a thousand
deaths enter ever new worlds to offer
my adoration to Thee.

1904
Se to se diner katha bakyahin jabe …
from 'Utsarga'

127

THE GOLDEN MOMENT

O mother, how can I attend to
humdrum household tasks today, when
the Prince of my dreams will pass by our
door this morning?

Rather, tell me in what way shall I
braid my hair, what garment must I put
on.

Why do you look at me amazed,
mother?

I know very well that he will not cast
a glance where I shall stand waiting; in
the flicker of an eye he will pass out of
my life, and only the last lingering notes
of the flute will come wailing across the
distant fields.

And yet, how can I help but bedeck
myself in the best of raiments, for the
brief moment it would take the Prince
charming to pass by our door?

O mother, the Prince of my dreams
did pass by our door.

The morning sun glittered on the
gold canopy of his chariot.

My veil swept aside, I did have a
glimpse of his face and tore the ruby
pendant from my chain and flung it on
his path.

128

Why do you look at me amazed,
mother?

I know full well that he did not pick
up my pendant, and the rubies were
crushed under the wheel; all that is left
are the tracks of his chariot in front of
our door.

What I gave and for whom shall for
ever remain a secret buried in roadside
dust.

And yet, how could I help but tear
the jewel from my breast and fling it
before his path, for the Prince charming
did pass by our door?

July, 1905
Subhakhayan from 'Kheya'

IN THE MORNING

It rained all night long. Overnight, my little pond became a brimful lake. When I awoke I saw water everywhere—blue and deep and brinkless. It is a wonder how one night's rain made a brimful lake of my little pond.

Last night the rain came and it poured without cease through the dark hours. I little knew then this miracle would happen. As I lay in my lampless room, shrouded by the *Sravana* night, listening to the wind moaning across the fields, I little knew this miracle would come to pass.

And now, look, on the fathomless sea of my tears, floats a snow-white lotus—one lonely lotus, bright and full-blown and gleeful in the sun. Who can tell when the lotus bloomed in the fathomless sea of my tears?

As I sit by myself and gaze at the lotus, I wonder at the blossom out of the sad heart of my night of sorrow. Out of all my heart breaks, out of the tears that I shed through the wakeful hours, out of my sighs that the gusty wind scattered, arose this one lotus, white and chaste, out of the sad heart of my night of sorrow.

July, 1905
Prabhate from 'Kheya'

130

THE PORTRAIT

*A*re you only a portrait on canvas limned?
Those distant nebulae which crowd together
in the nest of the sky; the sun, the moon, the
stars that travel day and night through the
dark with lighted torches; are you not as real
as they?
    Alas you are a picture, only a portrait.

    Amid the ever-restless, why do you stay fixed?
    Join the wayfarers, O pathless one. Night
and day why are you so distant while with us
all, sequestered in eternal stillness?
    This dust swirls the veil of greyness and flies
upon the wind in all directions; in *Vaisakh* it
divests the widowed Earth of all adornment
and dresses her in the ochre robes of the
devotee; in the glad dawn of spring decorates
her with verdant bloom. Ah yes, this dust is
also real.
    These blades of grass lying at the foot of the
world,—they are restless, they are real.
    You are still, you are a picture, you are only
a portrait.

    One day you walked beside us on the road,
your bosom moved with your breath, your life
surged through your body in song and dance and
created its own rhythms in tune with the world;
    That day is long ago.

In this life in my world how real you were.
In my eyes you were the one in the Universe;
on every side you drew with the brush of
beauty the image of delight. You were in that
dawn the world's speech incarnate.

As we walked together on the road, you
stopped and were hidden by the night. I went
on by night and by day through many sorrows,
many joys.
Daylight and dark, ebbtide and flood
continue in the ocean of the sky. On both
sides of the road the flowers march, treading
silently, many hued. Life's fountain rushes
headlong in a thousand streams sounding the
anklets of death.

Following the call of the unknown I have
gone from distance to distance, intoxicated by
the joy of the road.
You stood still where you had stepped aside.
This grass, this dust, those stars, that moon
and sun,— beyond them all you are a picture,
you are only a portrait.

What mad words of a poet are these? Are
you a picture? Not so, not so, you are not a
mere picture.
Who shall say that you are moveless,
prisoned in lines in silent weeping?
Alas, if that joy which once was should cease
to be, this river would lose the impulse of its

132

waves, this cloud would wipe out its golden writ.

If the sheen of your dark hair were to disappear from the world, then one day, the rustling, resonant shadows of the *Madhavi*–forest would be but a dream.

Did I ever forget you? But you have made your home at the heart of life—So this illusion.

Absent-minded I walk, do I not forget the flowers or the stars? And yet they make sweet the breath of life, filling forgetfulness with their music.

To remain unremembering is not oblivion; sitting in the secret heart of forgetfulness, you stir my blood.

You are not before my eyes, you dwell at the centre of my sight; and so, today, you are the green of the green, the blue of the blue. My world has found in you its inmost harmony.

I do not know, no one knows your music resounds in my song; in the heart of the poet you are the poet. You are not a picture, you are not a mere portrait.

I found you one morning, then lost you in the night. Then in the dark, unknowingly, I win you again and again. You are not a picture, you are not a mere picture.

October, 1914
Chhabi from 'Balaka'

SHAH JEHAN

*Y*ou knew, Shah Jehan, life and youth, wealth
and glory, they all drift away in the current of
time. You strove, therefore, to perpetuate only
the sorrow of your heart.

Kingly power, stern as thunder, may sink
into sleep like the glowing embers of the
setting sun. Be that as it may, let one long sigh
soar for evermore and envelop the sky with
sadness,—that was the longing of your heart.
Let the splendour of diamond, pearl and ruby
vanish like the magic shimmer of the rainbow.
Only let this one tear-drop, this *Tajmahal*,
glisten spotlessly bright on the check of time,
for ever and ever.

Alas for the human heart, it has no time at
all to look back on any one. The boat of life
rushes along the swift current of time, from
one landing place to another, from one mart to
another, loading and unloading.

Urged by the murmur of the soft South
wind, no sooner does the tender *madhavi* come
into bloom and fill with flowers the skirt of the
spring, the twilight of parting comes, and
strews the petals in the dust. But there is no
time to lament. And so in the nights washed
with dew, the bowers laugh with new blown

kunda flowers to fill autumn's basket with
tearful joy.

Alas, O heart, you must leave by the
roadside, morning and evening, all that you
had garnered, for there is no time, none at all.

So with fearful heart, O King, you sought to
charm time with the magic of beauty and
weave a garland that would bind formless
death with deathless form.

There is no time here to mourn for ever
more. So you bound fast your disconsolate cry
in the coils of a timeless silence. And now
eternity listens to your whispered voice, calling
your beloved by the name you murmured in
the privacy of your chamber on a moonlit
night. The tenderness of your love is now
engraved as flowers on the silent stone.

Poet-king, this is the image of your heart,
your new epic, your cloud messenger. Its song
and rhythm ascend towards the unseen where
your lone beloved has become one with the
roseate promise of the dawn, with the weary
sigh of the desolate evening and the
incorporeal sweetness of the jasmine under the
full moon; where speech reaches not and
yearning eyes come back baffled.

Even to this bourne does your courier of
beauty repair, from age to age, eluding the

watch of time, carrying your wordless message:
'Never shall I forget you, beloved, never.'

O King, you are no more. Your empire has vanished like a dream, your throne lies shattered, your cohorts—under whose marching feet the very earth trembled—have become a memory blown about in Delhi's dusty winds.

Your minstrels sing no more, your musicians no longer mingle their strains with the murmuring Jamuna. The ankle-bells of your palace dancers have yielded place to the cry of cicadas in the dusty corners of your ruined courts. Their plaintive moans fill the night sky with sadness.

Despite all this, the courier of your love, untarnished by time, unwearied, unmoved by the rise and fall of empires, unconcerned with the ebb and flow of life and death, carries the ageless message of your love from age to age:
'Never shall I forget you, beloved, never.'

Vain and false your protestation.
Who says you did not forget, that you never opened the doors of memory's cage? Is your heart still enclosed in the eternal night of the past? Has it not sought deliverance through oblivion's path?

The mausoleum stands still and unmoving in its place. Here on the dusty earth, it keeps death tenderly covered in the shroud of memory.

Who can keep life in chains? The stars, each and one, call out to life: worlds beyond worlds—each with its own sun arising out of a new horizon—offer life their welcome.

Life cuts asunder the knot of memory and ranges all over the universe—free of all bonds.

O mighty emperor, not the mightiest of empires could hold you, nor could the ocean-girdled world contain you. At the end of life's feast, you spurned this earth like the used clay cup that is kicked aside.

You are greater than what your hands had fashioned; the chariot of your life courses forward,—leaving behind your own creation. Only your symbol remains, but you are here no more.

The love that is static, the love that does not move forward made for itself a throne of grandeur in the middle of the road. The cloying sweetness of that love was like so much dust that clung to your feet.

You have shaken it off and returned dust into dust.

In to the dust you left behind, a chance wind brought a seed from life's garland,—an idea born in your soul.

You have now moved far ahead, but out of that seed has sprouted a deathless message—a voice that ascends ever higher and sings in solemn notes:

'However far I may gaze, I see no trace of the traveller who was here. His beloved could not hold him back, his empire made way for him, neither sea nor mountains could impede his progress. The night called out to him and the stars of the heavens sang to him. His chariot sweeps along towards the portals of a new dawn. It is I who am left behind, borne down by memory's burden while he, the unfettered one, is here no more!'

October, 1914
E katha janite tumi Bharateshwar Shah Jehan . . .
from 'Balaka'

THE UNRESTING

O Ye vast River! your waters, mute and
    invisible, flow unimpeded, flow on for ever!

The voids of Space vibrate under your mighty
    incorporeal speed.
The tremendous impact of your Matterless
    stream wakes up masses of foamy Matter.
Beams of piercing light rush out of darkness
    and spurt into torrents of spectrum.
Minute as bubbles, the sun, the moon, the
    stars, each in its own sphere rotates round
    and round in that cosmic whirl!

O *Bhairavi*! O All-Renouncer! the inarticulate
    tunes of your music are but the rhythm of
    your goalless march.
Does the lure of illimitable distance rouse you
    to a perennial response?
Does its ruinous love make you eternally the
    homeless wanderer?
As you move towards your wild love tryst, the
    necklace of stars on your breast shivers and
    breaks and scatters like gems.
Darkling in the unending spaces your storm-
    beaten unruly hair stretches like a streamer.
The lightning, your ear-ring, gleams; and the
    skirts of your garment trail along the
    trembling grass and along the shivering
    flower-groves of a million woodlands.

As you move on and on, what an abundance
of flowers *juin*, *champak*, *bakul* and *parul*,
drop down from the seasons on your tray!

Rush on, rush on, only rush on in your wild
uncontrollable speed!
You cast no lingering look behind but shed off
all that is yours.
You pick up nothing, you never hoard, you
have no regret, no fear, freely you spend
your all in the joy of sheer motion!

The moment of fulfilment is the moment of
nullity for you and therefore you are
constantly pure.
At the touch of your feet, the dust of the
universe forgets its taint.
Death itself is transformed into life and surges
upward.
Were you to halt for a moment for weariness,
the universe would explode into splinters of
congregated Matter.
Dreadful masses of dumb stagnant shapeless
darkness would retard all mobility, and even
the atoms and molecules, weighed down by
their delirious burden of accumulating
immobility, would be pierced with the pang
of defilement!

Invisible Dancer! quick-limbed Maiden!
Your life-giving cosmic rhythm pours constantly like
the waters of the river of heaven, the *Mandakini*,

and purifies the life of the universe by bathing it
in death.
An inexhaustible spotless blue pervades the all-
encompassing sky.

The resistless spontaneous march of the music-
vibrant universe fills you, O Poet, with yearning.
The echoes of the footfall of the Unresting can
be heard in your veins and your heart is
resonant in unison.
No one knows that in your blood today is the
swell of sea-waves, that the yearning of the
forest stirs within you.
I remember how from aeon to aeon I have
glided imperceptibly from form to form,
from one shape of vitality to another;
how all that I came by, morning and evening.
I spent in unremitting largess, in songs without end!

And look, the tide now runs high and articulate.
Your boat trembles.
Let all that you hoarded ashore be now left
behind, Glance not back.
Let the call of what is to be impel you forward
to the great stream from the tumult behind
to an unplumbed darkness, an illimitable
effulgence!

December, 1914
He birat nadi, adrishaya nishshabda taba jal . . .
from 'Balaka'

FLYING CRANES

*G*littering in the evening glow the curving
current of the Jhelum paled in the darkness,
shut in a sheath like a scimitar. The flood of
night brought stars like flowers floating on its
black waters at the ebb of day. Beneath the
banks of darkening hills stood row on row of
deodars. It seemed as if in a dream creation
strove to speak but expression eluded her and
inarticulate words broke sobbing through the
gloom.

On a sudden that instant I heard through the
twilight heaven a flash of sound like lightning
across the field of space. A moment and it was
gone, distant and more distant still! O flying
cranes! Your wings, drunk with the wine of the
wind, heaping high joy's shrill laughter, awoke
waves of wonder in the sky. The sound of wings,
like a singing nymph of paradise, shattered the
penance of silence as it passed. The range of hills,
plunged in night, began to tremble; in unison
trembled the forest of deodars.

The summons of those wings seemed to bring
for an instant only to the thrilling heart of
stillness the shock of swift motion. The hills
longed to wander like clouds in spring, trees
wished to put on wings and abandon earthly ties
and lose themselves along the line of sound,
searching for the shores of the sky. As this dream

of evening dimmed, there beat aching waves of
yearning for the faraway. O far seeking wings, a
passionate cry broke from creation's lips: 'Not
here! Not here! but somewhere else.'

O flying cranes! Tonight, you took away for
me the covering from silence. Beneath the
hush I hear a sound of wings, eager and wild,
on land and sea and sky. The grass flaps its
wings on the spread-out earth, flocks of seeds
in millions sprout tender wings in the sub-
terranean dark. I can see this range of hills and
these forests soar with wings outspread from
land to land, from one unknown to beyond.
The darkness throbs with crying light in the
pulsing wings of stars.

I heard the many voiced words of man wing
along unheeded ways, from the faded past to
far off future dim. I heard within myself the
sound of this homeless bird winging with
countless other birds from shore to shore
through daylight and darkness. Space echoes
with the song of all creation's wings: 'Not
here! Elsewhere! Elsewhere! Somewhere else!'

October, 1915
Sandhaya rage jhilimili Jhilumer srotkhani banka . . .
from 'Balaka'

TWO WOMEN

*A*t the churning of primeval seas at the hour
   of creation, there arose two women from
   the unplumbed sea-bed;
Urvashi, the beautiful, the queen of desire, the
   dancer of heaven;
and Lakshmi, the blessed one, the mother of
   the universe, the lady of heaven.

The One disrupts the ascetic's meditation, and
   with loud laughter steals his heart and soul,
serving him with fire-filled tankards of Spring-
   time wine, scattering with both hands the
   flowery delirium of Spring;
passion-red roses and unslumbering songs of youth.

The other laves you with dewy tears and turns
   you back to tender yearnings,
to the fullness of the golden peace of fruit-
   laden autumn;
brings you back to the blessings of the
   universe, to the sweet serene smile of
   unwavering grace;
gently brings you back to the sacred
   confluence of life and death,
      to the temple of the infinite.

February, 1915
Kon khane srijaner saumdramanthane . . . from 'Balaka'

144

THE DECEPTION

*B*inu was twentythree when she fell ill.
Doctors and medicines surrounded her—phials
and bottles, square pill-boxes and round—till
the remedy seemed a greater burden than the
malady. After a year and a half of this strain
the doctors declared, 'She must have a
change.' So it came about that Binu boarded a
railway carriage for the first time, and for the
very first time after her marriage came out of
her in-law's house.

In the closer intimacy of a joint family, it
was only occasionally we could meet, furtively
and for a few brief moments. Like two
disconnected themes which met only to come
away, our relationship was a patchwork of half-
completed sentences, laughter cut short. Today
the Earth gathered into her arms the light from
all her surrounding skies and wrapped it in
benediction about the groom and bride. There
was a new-found joy in Binu's eyes—grown
enormous in her wasted face—as if she looked
anew at her love on a new bridal night.

Binu threw open her cash box, and
plunging her hand in, flung coins, whatever
she could find, quarters or whole, to the
beggars as at the end of the day they crossed

145

the railway line. If all sorrows could not be removed, how could happiness, such as hers, take architectural shape and bear its own weight? Our journey had become a voyage of joy, away from the crowded banks of daily life and had to find fulfilment in gifts and munificence for all. A thought seemed to have risen in Binu's mind that in this whole wide world only I was her very own. Cousins, brothers, aunts, and in-laws, they belonged to another world, and this thought brought a glow, a new urgency, to her being.

We had to change trains at Bilaspur. Quickly we got down and discovered we had six long hours to wait. I thought it was an infliction but Binu protested, 'Oh no, what is so tiresome about it?' There was no end to her happiness today, for the journey's song had brought the rhythm of dance to her feet; her joy had blended arrival and voyaging into a unity.

She opened the door of the waiting room and cried, 'Look, look at that funny cart. There's a calf, how velvet, tender-smooth its body, how deep the love in its mother's eyes. There, by the high bank of the pond is a small house under the shade of the tall *Shishu* tree surrounded by guarding walls—who lives there, the Station Master? How comfortably they live.'

I spread her bed in the waiting-room and told Binu, 'Lie down now and sleep.' Then

146

outside, on the platform, I pulled out a chair and settled down to read an English novel I had brought. Some three hours had passed, trains roared through, goods and express, when Binu came out of the waiting-room and said, 'I want a word with you.'

I came into the waiting-room and found a Northern Indian woman who saluted me and walked out to stand against a verandah pillar. Binu said, 'Her name is Rukmini, and there, near the well, where that row of small hutments are, is where she lives. Her husband is a porter at the Station here. In—I don't know which year, nineteen something or the other—there was a failure of crops, and these two, the husband and wife, fled to escape the landlord's wrath. They had seven *bighas* of land in some village on the banks of some river, and . . .' I laughed and cut her short, 'Our train will arrive before you end Rukmini's story. It will do no harm if you gave me a briefer version.' Binu knit her brows and with offended eyes said, 'Certainly not, why should I tell it to you in brief? Today there is no office to attend. You will have to listen to the story from its very beginning to the end.' My mood for the novel evaporated and I had to concentrate on the tale of the railway porter—spread out before me in all its biographical detail.

The point of the story was right at the end and it was a costly business. The couple had a

marriageable daughter and had to find anklets,
a necklet, and silver clasps for her marriage.
After hard bargainings and severest economies,
there was still a shortage of twentyfive rupees.
This was making Rukmini distracted.
Therefore, before entraining and going away, it
was up to me to give her this money, and
remove the worry of the railway porter's wife.

The demand and conclusion amazed me—
the situation was incredible . . . Here was a
woman, by occupation low, by caste possibly
untouchable, a woman who earned her living
by cleaning and sweeping the waitingroom,
and I was to give her twentyfive rupees for her
daughter's marriage. Should this become a
habit, it would not be many days before we
would have to face the insolvency court.
To quieten Binu I said, 'Yes, quite, quite, I
will see to it all, but I have only one hundred
rupee note and no change.' Binu countered,
'You can change it at the Station.' 'Yes, yes, of
course, I will see to it,' I said and called the
woman to one side. I gave her a scolding, 'I
will have you dismissed for cheating a
passenger and put an end to your mischief.' It
was only when she fell weeping at my feet that
I relented and dismissed her with two rupees.
The light went out in the mansion of my
life. Two months later when I returned to

148

Bilaspur, I was alone. Before she died, Binu touched my feet and said, 'I may forget all else in my life, but these last two months I have spent with you will live for ever in my memory. They shall endure like the vermilion that Narayani, the goddess, puts on the parting of her hair. You have filled with sweetness these last two months. I shall always remember this as I bid you farewell.'

Oh Lord of our inmost thoughts, I want to tell Binu that in the festival of love of the last two months, there was no great gap: the twentyfive rupees I did not give. Even if I pay Rukmini a hundred thousand rupees today, it will not settle that account of deception. Binu will not know that these last two months that she felt I had given her as a loving gift were not complete because of this one denial.

To my anxious enquiries at Bilaspur, 'Where is Rukmini?' people answered, 'Who is she?' Not many knew her and it was only when I said, 'That woman, Jhumroo coolie's wife,' that some one said, 'They have left.' 'Where shall I find them?' I asked, and the Station Master angrily said, 'Who knows where such people go.' The ticket clerk smiled and said, 'A month ago they left, it may have been for Darjeeling, or Khusroobagh, or the Arakans.' The more I asked, the more they were annoyed, for who would bother about such small people?

How can I explain, how shall I make them understand, that these, the most unimportant, have become for me the most valued. It is this Rukmini alone who can remove the blot of my deception. How shall I rest when in my ears ring Binu's words, 'You filled with sweetness these last two months'? I shall now for ever remain a debtor, for my deception has become immutable.

October, 1917
Fanki from 'Palataka'

SUNDAY

*M*onday Tuesday Wednesday always come in
 such a rush,
I think their families all have got the latest
 motor cars.
But, Mummy, tell me why does Sunday always
 lag behind,
Arriving here so slowly after all the other days?
Is his house farther than the others, way
 beyond the skies?
Perhaps his family's poor like yours, Mummy,
 and can't afford a car.

Monday Tuesday Wednesday simply do not
 want to leave,
Their mind is set on staying here and never
 going home.
But who is packing Sunday off in such a
 dreadful hurry?
They seem to ring the hour-bell after every
 half an hour.
Does he have much more work to do at home
 beyond the skies?
Perhaps his family's poor like yours, Mummy,
 and can't afford a maid.

Monday Tuesday Wednesday have black faces
 like a saucepan's bottom!

151

And with us little children they are not on
    speaking terms.
But when I wake up in the morning after
    Sat'day night,
I see a smile on Sunday's face—a smile that
    stays all day.
And when the time comes to part, he looks in
    our faces and cries.
Perhaps his family's poor like yours, Mummy,
    he looks so sad.

September, 1921
Rabibar from 'Bholanath'

FULLNESS

I

One still night, moved by sleepless passion,
you said, with bowed head and tearful eyes,
gently kissing my hand—
'If you go away, my universe, weighed down
by the burden of unending emptiness, will turn
into a desert, wholly dreary;
'Sky-wide weariness will denude my soul of
all peace. Congealed grief, joyless and lustreless,
will bring death worse than death.'

II

At that, I pressed your face against my
breast and whispered—
'If you go far from me, my soul will shimmer
from moment to moment in tune with the
lightning pangs of your songs. The experience
of separation will play its many-coloured game
on my being.'
'You will discover, dear, from your distance,
the door closest to my soul. And then o'er my
universe will fulfil itself your ultimate
sovereignty.'

III

The whispered dialogue of the two was
heard by the Seven Stars. The liquid words

153

trembled through the scented groves of
rajanigandha.

And then stealthily, an impassable
separation yawned between the two in the
shape of death. We meet no more; words
ceased in an infinite bereft of touch.

And yet the void is no vacuum, for its skies
are filled with fiery clouds of grief; and in my
loneliness, I create in glowing songs a world of
dreams out of their flame.

October, 1924
Purnata from 'Purabi'

154

THE FLEETING ONE

*R*emove the silent blue curtain, o sky, let me search
for that lost fragment of joy.

On a day long past at the turn of time she had
entered my heart: A traveller of twilight hour, she
came to this desolate field of mine holding a lamp
with a timorous flame. And then I know not where
she, my fleeting one, moved away beyond the far
horizon.

I thought I had forgotten, thought that the
faithless devouring dust had covered her footprints
step by step. But today I feel how that faint footfall
has captured the rhythm of my song, see how her
invisible fingers still make ripples in the lake of tears.

Separation brought that dying lamp and left it in
an unknown chamber of my heart. A *veena* lying
there woke to fleeting music at a sudden stroke; but
through the silent nights since then the goddess
with the *veena*, on a lotus of pain has searched for
the music that died in the dark.

She had hid herself in a shadowy veil that by her
impatience she could not remove. Her timid eyes
vanished with their mystery behind the veil of piled-
up darkness. Ever in my dreams I try to lift that veil
and ponder the mystery that lay in the dark depths
of her startled eyes.

If you had not fled startled, self-forgetful one, if you had only stopped and looked back, the silent tingled night would have revealed the final intent of two lives. Then in that ultimate hour, my friend, your lamp's transient flame would have lit the expanse of eternity.

Traveller, I now look into the dust of the road you trod. The denied moment lies there—your gift. Gazing at the writing of the unfulfilled, I know not if you intended to leave some sign. The broken flower, was it false pretence? I wanted to ask, but the time is gone.

The shadowy veil remains. In the twilight haze of not-knowing, the fitful image of dreams makes my shining eyes drunk with doubt and enchantment. The image flits about me, mingled in shadow and light, yet remains infinitely far in illusion's drowsy realm. The mirage of the unknown wails for the fleeting one.

Remove the silent blue curtain, o sky. I will search among the stars for the jewels of her necklace. I will search in the realms whence comes *Aswin's** brief twilight glow, whence descends to earth the jasmine of a *Sravan*† evening, whence rushes the storm with lightning's momentary flash.

6 October, 1924
Kshanika from 'Purabi'

---

* *Aswin*: an autumn month.
† *Sravan*: a month in the rainy season.

156

THE LAST SPRING

Before this day ends let my wish be granted:
  Let us for the last time go out together to
pick the flowers of spring.
  Many *Falgoons* will visit your garden, I want
just one.

  I was not aware so long how the days had
passed.
  And then in your eyes in the evening light
I suddenly saw my day was about to end.
  So like a miser, restless, hesitant, I count the
last days of my spring.

  Do not be afraid: I shall not tarry too long
in your blooming garden.
  I shall not look back in vain at this sunset
hour of parting.
  I shall not look for tears in your eyes nor
want you to remember me for ever with pity.

      Do not go back, listen, oh listen!
      The sun has not yet set, there is still
          time.
      Do not hesitate to deceive time a little.
      Let the afternoon glow from behind the
      leaves sparkle for a while on your dark
          black hair.

  Break out into sweet laughter and in a
sudden rush of cruel joy, scare the timid

157

শেষ অংশ

আসিবেন   দিন যে

হবে মোর এ আশা পূরাতে,—

শুধু এবারের মতো

বসন্তের ফুল যত

ধরা মোরা দুর্বল কুড়াতে।

তোমার কারবলপথে ফুলবন আসিবে ভরমার,

তাহারি একটি শুধু সাধি আমি দুয়ারে তোমার ॥

তবে করে ফিরে যাব

এবারের ফুল কিছু তুলি ভূমিতে ফিরিব সে কয়টি।

হয়তো তোমার চোখে

দেখি সত্যলোক

এমন সময় আর নাই।

তাই আমি রসে রসে সমিতিতি কুসুমের সম

এসব সাজীতে ভরে বসন্তের দিনগুলি মম ।

ভয় রাখিয়ো না তুমি মনে,

তোমার বিষ্ণু ফুলবনে

দেরি করিবনা মিছে,

দিরে চাহিবনা পিছে

দিনশেষে বিদায়ের ক্ষণে ।

158

squirrel on the pond's edge in the wood.

I shall not slow down your impatient feet by talking of those forgotten days.

You can then go away, crushing the fallen leaves with your quick feet when the homing bird twitters and disturbs the twilight hour.

In the shadows your image will merge with the last notes of twilight song.

When it grows very dark you will sit at your window.

And beloved, I shall leave all and take to the road, never to meet again.

You can throw away the white garland you wore at dawn.

That will be your last touch, your parting word.

21 November, 1924
Shesh Basanta from 'Purabi'

BEHOLDEN

*F*orget you? Never!' I had said when, on
tear's brink, your eyes, wordless, held my face.

Forgive me if I have forgotten.

Years have gone since that day's caress.

Many a spring has passed in between, its
madhavi blooming in bunches and fading off
again, and multitudes of days have come and
gone, weighed by the tired slumber that dove-
song brings at noon.

Your dark eyes with shy and shrinking glances
had scrolled in my soul the first epistle of love.

Over the signature of your heart has passed
the brush of time, fitful with the light and
shade of passing hours.

Many an evening has painted on it the
molten gold of oblivion, many a night has
covered it over with its alphabet of dreams in a
maze of unclear lines!

Like a lad who hath no care, each moment
is busy, always and meanderingly, drawing
memory's lines on the canvas of the mind,
weaving a web of forgetfulness.

If in today's spring-time I have forgotten the
voice of an earlier *Phalgoon*, forgive me.

If, unnoticed, the flame has gone out of my
lamp of pain, forgive me.

160

Yet this I know, that it was only because
you came that my life was filled with a harvest
of songs, a harvest that yet knows no end.

The light in your eyes stole out of sunbeams
the secret in their core and made music of it all.

Your touch is no longer with me, but in my
being you've left a touch-stone that again and
again fills with sweetness the picture of our
world,—

Fills, without cause, the bowl of joy out of
which I might drink.

Forgive me then if I have forgotten.

Do I not know that you had called me
once to your heart?

I can pardon my fate for all the sorrow and
sadness stacked into my days.

From my parched lips Fate has snatched the
cup, it has piled deception, with a smirk
broken faith, drowned a full boat within sight
of the shore.

All these I forgive.

No longer with me, you're farther than far away.

The vermilion wiped off your hair's parting
has left the very evening desolate.

Alone, I dwell in a house bereft of beauty.

All this I know, but most of all I know that
one day you and I were together.

2 November, 1924
Kritagya from 'Purabi'

HOMAGE TO THE TREE

*D*eep down under the earth you heard the
call of the sun in your dark chamber and felt
    the first stir of consciousness.
O Tree, O primal spring of life, you raised your
head above the passive rock and uttered the
    first prayer in praise of light.
The harsh and sapless desert got from you its
    first sensation.

On that day, in varied tones and hues, you
declared the glory of this earth to the
firmament with its assemblage of stars and
    planets.
Facing the great unknown, you held aloft the
victorious banner of life—of life that crosses
the mighty gate of death age after age and in
ever-new chariots hurries on to make its
    pilgrimage on ever-new paths.

At your silent call the earth woke up. Her
    dream was broken.
She quivered and recalled her own chronicle.
A reckless daughter of the gods, dressed in
lowly rags and smeared with ash, she sought
the bliss of heaven, wandering through
    fragments of space and time.
She longed to shatter that bliss with blows of
strife and pain for the pleasure of making it
    whole again.

Valiant offspring of the dust, you waged a
continuous war to liberate the earth from the
        fortress-prison of aridity.
Mounted on the ocean's soaring wave you
reached distant islands, and on their barren
shores established the royal power of verdure
        with supreme confidence.
You scaled forbidding mountainsides and upon
their stony pages wrote an epic of victory in
        leafy alphabet.
You charmed the dust, and fashioned for
yourself in trackless regions a web of verdant
        paths.
There was a day when all were dumb—the earth,
the oceans and the empty vault of heaven—
        while the seasons knew no music.
You came, and your tuneful branches brought
comfort to the world. In your melody the
restless wind first discovered itself,
painted its own invisible body with varied hues
of sound, and etched the rainbow of song
        upon the sky.

On the earth's canvas you were the first to sketch
the living image of beauty. From the sun you
extracted its formative power, fused it with your
own breath, and scattered the treasure of light in
        countless colours.
One day the nymphs of Indra's heavenly court
struck the clouds with their jingling bracelets,

broke those jars of vapour, and in playful dance
　　　　poured out the wine of youth.
You saved that nectar in your leaves and flowers,
and with them you beautified the earth, making
　　　　her eternally young.

O Tree, O silent solemn tree, it was you who
first joined patience to valour and showed how
　　　　power can incarnate itself in peace.
I take refuge in you. Initiate me into the
fellowship of tranquillity, that I may hear the
　　　　profound message of silence.
I bend my head, burdened with anxious
thoughts, and touch the dust in your soothing
　　　　shade.
There I seek the varied forms of Life: the
generous form, the form of ever-new joys, the
heroic form, splendid, world-conquering, and
　　　　the eloquent form which the earth displays.

I have meditated, entered into your spirit, have
understood how the sun—the holy flame that
burns for the sacrificial ritual of creation—
through your being silently assumes a glossy,
　　　　tender form.
O Tree, O sunbeam-quickened, for centuries
you milked the days—as though they were
white cows—and the vigour acquired
from this nourishment you gave away to
　　　　mankind as a gift.

With your own strength you made man
invincible, raised him to the pitch of honour
    until he dared to rival the gods.
And now his flaming power breaks all barriers
    while the universe stares in deep amazement

From the realm of man I come to you, O Tree,
    as a messenger.
I speak for him—for man who is animated by
your breath, who rests in your cool loving
    shade, who wears your flowery garland.
O friend of man, I am a poet charmed by your
music, and I bring to you with humble
    greetings this verse-offering.

March, 1927
Brikhaya Vandana from 'Banabani'

THE LADY OF THE SEA

*Y*ou bathed in the sea and sat on the pebbled
   shore with wet untied hair.
Your loose yellow dress rested on the damp soil
   in curved lines around you.
On your uncovered breasts and unadorned
   body the dawn wrote its fond message in
   lines of gold.
On my brow there shone the dragon crown, in
   my right hand I held my bow.
I came before you in royal robes and said, 'A
   stranger, I have come to your shore.'

Startled, you stood up from your seat of stone
   and asked, 'Why have you come?'
I said, 'Do not be afraid, I only want to gather
   from your garden flowers for my God.'
You smiled your consent and walked by my side.
Together we plucked the *junthee* and the *jatee*
   and the *champak*, together we arranged
   them in my prayer bowl, together we sat in
   worship of the Lord of Dance.
The mist disappeared and in the sky the light
   shone like the smile of Parvati as she gazed
   upon Shiva's face.

When the evening star rose over the mountain
   peak you were sitting alone in your room.

Your blue skirt was tied around your waist, garlands
    of *malati* were twined upon your head, the
    tingling bracelets clung to your wrists.
As I walked on the way I played on my flute, I
    came to your door and said, 'Look, here is a
    guest for you.'

Startled you quickly lit your lamp and looked
    at me, and asked, 'Why have you come?'
I replied, 'Do not fear, I have come only to
    deck with my jewels your slender limbs.'
You looked at me with a smiling face as I hung
    over your breasts a golden garland shaped
    like the crescent moon.
I took off my dragon crown and made it a
    circlet for your dusky hair.
Your maidens came and lit the lamps, the
    jewels on your body sparkled and shone.
The night of the spring became sweet and tender,
    your dance and my drum mingled in unison.
The full moon smiled on the cloudless sky, like
    Shiva and Shivani, light and shade
    trembled on the waters of the sea.

I do not know when the day came to an end.
    I launched my boat again in the gathering
    evening.
Suddenly the winds became contrary, with
    mighty waves Destruction ranged in
    the depth of the seas.

Filled with salt-water my rich ship foundered
    and sank in the dark night.

Today a man of broken fortunes, I stand again
    at your door shorn of ornaments and in
    torn and poor dress
I opened the gate of the temple of the Lord of
    Dance, I found that the bowls are still full
    of flowers as of old.
When with wild abandon and liquid music the
    moon started the dance of light upon the
    waters of the sea, I saw on your tender
    lowered face the decorations I had painted
    and on your heart the garland I had woven.
I saw with silent pleasure that the rhythm which I
    had once played on the *mridang* still moves your
    lovely limbs in fluent music and gentle sound.

Listen to me, O beauteous maiden, come once again
    before me with the lamp in your hand.
I no longer have on my head the dragon crown nor
    have I the bow and arrows in my hand.
Nor have I brought to you in your garden by the sea
    new gifts and offerings with the southern wind.
I have brought with me only my harp, look at
    me and see if you remember me.

1 October, 1927
Sagarika from 'Mahua'

THE RIDDLE

The one she loves—she loves to make him
weep. Each time a new enigma, she confounds
the image in his heart. Her light now shade, her
shade now light, contrives his constant doubt.
With great pretence of wounded pride she has
him on his knees. Like autumn's magic showers
from harmless-looking clouds, her glance suggests
encouragement, but lightning shoots behind.

Why with disconcerting laughter scatter a
lover's pleas? Then fall herself a victim of the
cruel game? With grieving heart to get back
whom she has turned away, she shatters into
pieces her own wounded vanity. Why in the
sky of her mind all day this wild madly
sporting wind? To want to go one way and yet
go the other, who can understand? Not she!

Deep in her mind, unknown to herself,
what conflict with herself? Her anger is against
herself and so she hurts another. But suddenly
with molten pity she is at his feet, pouring out
her heart and mind. Is her name, Heyali?*

July, 1928
Heyali from 'Mahua'

---

* The 'e' in Heyali has a nasal sound which cannot be transliterated without making use of
phonetic symbols: the nearest English equivalent is 'Riddle'.

THE ETERNAL

*A*long this foreign road my car speeds,
honking, veiling the sky with dust. At such a
time the cuckoo calls from a cool-branched
lemon tree, from the depth of the roadside
forest.

In the voice of the bird the tune of eternity
seems to fall on this day drop by drop. In my
childhood, gazing at the water on Ganga's
bank, I heard the cuckoo's song from the
village. Inexpressible for ever, my heart heard
in the tune: 'You are my beloved.'

The notes spread across the forest foliage,
mingled with the rustling of waters, and lost
themselves in the distant blue sky. Away from
home today, those notes I hear at the disturbed
road-side, hear them bring their message to the
flowers in the hidden branch. The cool peace
of the forest shade engages in an intimate
whisper with the morning light. In their
converse I hear it clearly and sweetly said: 'You
are my beloved.'

Right near goes on the strife. The knife of
deception cuts into the ribs to steal simple
trust. Malicious laughter wreaks complex
disaster. In despondent grief, I see worldwide

human terror sets ablaze men's homes in flames
of doom, covers the universe with the net of
greed. Who will save, I wonder, self-destroying
man in his blindness?

At such a time, suddenly, the cuckoo calls
from the tender shade of the flowering *Asoka*
tree. My heart is touched by peace which is
the earliest, peace which is at the very end.
Inexpressible for ever, this peace tells me—
'You are my beloved.'

18 October, 1927
Chirantan from 'Parisesh'

QUESTION

*F*rom age to age, O God, you have sent your
apostles to this pitiless world: And they
preached their gospel: 'Forgive all trespasses,
love all, and banish hate from all hearts.' They
claim our homage, time will not forget them,
and yet, my regard unavailing, I must turn
them back.

Have I not seen stealthy malice, in the
night's deceitful shadow, hurl death at the
helpless? Have I not seen Justice mourn,
wordless and desolate, when the strong flaunt
their unchecked crimes? Have I not seen
youth, in agony, rush madly to break their
head against the baffling cruelty of stone?

Today I am throttled, my flute has lost its
music. *Amavasya's** gloom has smothered my
world in a nightmare. And so, in tears, I ask,
'Have you forgiven them who poison your air
and blot out your light? Have you blessed
them with your love?'

December, 1931
Prashna from 'Parisesh'

---

* *Amavasya* : the moon's darkest phase.

WONDER

*O*nce again I wake up. The night withers. The universe shoots out petals. This is the wonder, unending.

So many continents have sunk, so many stars have lost lustre, and aeons have elapsed! World-conquerors have lost their identities in the shadowy fringe of wordy chronicles. Nations erected obelisks on blood-smeared mud but only to quench the hunger of the dust. Amid these vast ruins, today my brow wears once again the morning sun's mark, and that is the wonder unending!

I stand today in the vast hall of the starry heavens. I am one with the Seven Stars and with the mounts of the Himalayas. I am where the dramatic play of the wild fury of the sounding ocean breaks into frenzied waves. On the bark of this giant tree, this lord of the forest, are imprinted the signatures of centuries. It has witnessed the rolling down of many crowns, and under its shade I have the sanction to sit for another day.

And I know that within the womb of this day clatter the wheels of time invisible, inaudible.

June, 1932
Bishway from 'Parisesh'

173

THE JOURNEY

*T*he king sets out to war. Trumpets blow and
cymbals clash. The earth trembles. The
Minister casts his net of intrigue and states are
tied in complex knots. The stream of
commerce girdles the earth in tides high and
low. Ships of trade sail to the end of the seas.
Monuments are raised to the brave on heaps of
human skeletons. They lift their heads high
and their towers shriek at heaven. Scholars
strike again and again at learning's fortress,
hard of access behind the walls built of books.
Their fame travels to distant lands.

Here at the hamlet's edge the river flows in a
tired stream to the flat country's end. The small
boat carries the bride to another village far away.
The sun sets and the fields are silent on both
banks. The girl's heart quivers. On the dark
horizon slowly appears the evening star.

January, 1932
Yatra from 'Bichitrita'

THE VOICE OF ETERNAL FORM

*T*he evening descended before its time and, like a solar eclipse, enveloped the courtyard in its dark shadow. Some one shouted: 'Open the door.'

Life, who lived in the house, was startled. He clung desperately to the door and bolted it securely. From his choking throat came the words: 'Who are you?'

Like the rumbling of a cloud the answer was heard: 'I am the messenger of the Kingdom of Dust. I have come to collect the debt you owe. Pay up, it is due.'

The door-chain rattled, the walls shivered, the wind groaned in the house. Unearthly wings fluttered in the sky, and their sound was like the heartbeat of Night herself. Blow followed blow, the bolts came loose, the door lay broken.

Life asked with a shaking voice: 'O dust, cruel dust, what do you want of me?' The messenger said: 'I want your body.'

Life heaved a deep sigh and said: 'This body, this is where I have held my festival for many a long year. Every atom of this body vibrates with my dance, every vein throbs with my music. Will you disperse the revelry at one swift blow?

175

Will you smash the flute and break the drum into pieces? Ah, my body! Will your days sink into the darkness of unfathomable night?'

The messenger scoffed: 'Your body, that miserable thing! Burdened with debt? From dust it came, to dust it shall return.'

Life replied, 'You may realise the earth's debt, but why do you demand more?'

The messenger countered, 'Your body is pale and weary like the moon the fourteenth night of the dark fortnight. How can one demand more from it?'

Life retorted: 'Well, the dust may be yours . . . But not the Form . . . not the beauty. . .'

The messenger laughed loudly and mocked: 'Indeed! Then why don't you extricate the Form, and keep it while I take the body away?'

Life said: 'I can and will. I accept your challenge.'

Life's friend, Mind, intervened. He made a pilgrimage to the sacred source of light. With folded hands he said: 'O mighty flame, O Eternal Light, O primal spring of Form! Let not your truth be shamed, let not your creation be slighted, by brute Matter. What right has he to destroy Form and make me suffer?'

With these words, Mind embarked upon a long, harsh penance. A thousand years passed,

176

a million years but Life's suffering did not end. On every path that he trod, he was waylaid, he was robbed of Form. The entire creation prayed for him, day and night: 'O Maker of Form, O Enjoyer of Form, the demon of Matter is taking away what you gave us as a gift. Arise, bring back your own treasure.'

Ages went by. Then one day a voice from heaven said: 'Let the earth's rightful property go back to the earth. Let the Form remain. I grant this boon: Form shall be recovered. The shadow shall be freed from the body. Arm in arm with light, she will attend your festival of creation.'
And so Form returned to the bodiless image. Conchshells were blown; lovers of Form came from every direction.

Again days passed, years passed. Life's mourning did not end—what is it now he wants?
With folded hands Life said: 'The messenger of Dust harasses me. His cruel hands choke my throat. He says: 'Your windpipe belongs to me.' I reply: 'The earthen reed may be yours, but the music is mine.' But he only mocks and laughs at me. O Universal Voice, hear my wailing, come to my aid. Will arrogant Dust be victorious? Will you allow blind, dumb matter to inflict eternal dumbness upon the living

word and erect Dust's tower of victory on your deathless message?'

Once again the heavenly voice was heard: 'Have no fear. In the ethereal ocean there are countless waves of Voices Unheard. Nothing is lost. I pronounce this benediction: Mind's penance shall bear fruit. The worn-out throat may be dissolved in the dust, but speech imperishable shall remain.'

What the demon of Matter had kidnapped in the chariot of Dust, Mind reclaimed. The fugitive gospel was enshrined in disembodied music.

The Cosmos reverberated with shouts of victory. On the bank of the river of Life, in the pavilion of existence, Bodiless Form was wedded to Bodiless Voice.

1932
Chiraruper Bani from 'Punashcha'

THE FIRST WORSHIP

The temple of Trilokeshwar—men say the divine architect himself laid its foundation in some far-distant past. The scholars of history say the temple was built by Kirats, and the deity in it was a Kirat god.

In course of time, a Kshatriya king conquered their land, and the temple courtyard flowed with the blood of their priests. The god was spared and lived on in another name under cover of new rites of worship. The ancient faith of a thousand years came to an end, the stream flowed in a new channel. The Kirats became untouchables, their entry to the temple forbidden.

The Kirats lived as outcastes in the area to the east of the river. They had no temple now, but they had their songs, and skilful hands and unerring sight. They knew how to bind stone to stone, to grave silver flowers upon brass, to shape images out of black stone. In administration they had no hand, their weapons were seized and taken away. In dress and dwelling and demeanour, they were reft of all dignity and honour, nor had they right to the knowledge of books.

Far to the west they saw the gold pinnacle of Trilokeshwar temple, saw in it the image of their heart's desire, and bowed to it from afar.

The Kartik *puja* was on a full-moon night; the festivities had commenced. On the platform over the gateway, the pipes played to the accompaniment of drum and cymbals. A city of tents rose on the fields and flags fluttered in the sky.

On both sides of the road were stalls with varied wares: copper vessels, silver ornaments, pictures of deities, cloths of silk, toy, wooden drums, earthen dolls, trumpets made of leaves, fruits and garlands, incense sticks, pots filled with water from holy shrines. The juggler pattered away as he showed his tricks, the story-teller chanted stories from the *Ramayana*, the armed guards rode among the crowd, clad in their splendid dress. The king's minister came, seated on an elephant, and heralded by trumpets.

Rich ladies came in palanquins draped with cloth of gold and retinues of servants before and behind. The *sannyasis* crowded beneath the sacred trees, with long matted hair, their naked bodied daubed with ashes; the women brought them offerings of fruits and milk and sweets, *ghee* and sun-dried rice. From time to time the cry rose to the skies: 'Glory to Trilokeshwar! To Trilokeshwar victory!'

Next day, at the auspicious hour, the king would come on the royal elephant and make his first oblation to the god. On the sides of the highway were planted banana trees decked with flowers. Mango twigs with leaves hung from auspicious water-pots, and scented water was sprinkled on the road.

It was two nights before the full-moon. In the temple the conches and gongs and kettle-drums had ushered in the first watch of the night. The moon was covered by a cloudy veil, its light hazy. The wind had stopped, the sky looked full of smoke; the distant trees were struck with awe; the dogs howled, why no one knew; the horses pricked up their ears, and neighed, seeking what others could not see.

Suddenly there was a deep and awful rumbling beneath the earth, as if monsters were beating their war-drums: Rub-a-dub, rub-a-dub! Loud and strident grew the sound of the temple gongs and conches. The elephants broke loose and, trumpeting, ran pell-mell. The earth shook and, wave-like, rolled.

The crowd stampeded in panic and cried for help, pushing and jostling and trampling on their own kith and kin. From fissures in the earth smoke rose, and hot water gushed up. The waters of the lake suddenly disappeared, sucked in by the sands. The big bell on the temple terrace swung to and fro, ringing out its peals till a crash was heard, when it suddenly stopped.

When the earth was quiet at last, the nigh-full moon had set to the west, smoke from

burning tents rose to the sky, like giant
pythons twined round the moonlight.

Next day all quarters were full of
lamentations, the king's soldiers formed a cordon
round the temple to preserve it from pollution.
The king's chief minister came, and the sooth-
sayer, and the *pundit* versed in religious rites.
They found the outer wall razed to the dust, and
the roof over the altar, collapsed.

The *pundit* said that the repairs must be
completed before the next full moon—or the
god would forsake the temple. The king
ordered that the repairs be carried out. His
minister said, 'Who can do the stone work but
the Kirats? And how is the god to be
protected from their impure gaze? What use
will the repairs be if the god is defiled?'

The king summoned the Kirat headman.
Old Madhav came, a pure white turban on his
silver hair and eyes filled with meekness and
humility. He bowed to the king from afar,
fearful lest his touch should pollute.

The king said, 'The temple repairs wait for
you.' 'That is the grace of the Lord on us,'
replied Madhav, and he bowed his head in
sign of reverence to the god.

The king said, 'Bandage your eyes as you work
that they may not fall upon the deity. Can you

work so?' Said Madhav, 'He who is within me will make me work. By my inner vision's light, I will not open my eyes as long as I work.'

The other Kirats worked outside the temple, Madhav worked within, his eyes bound by fold on fold of black cloth. Day and night he worked, praying and singing while his fingers moved.

The minister came and said, 'Make haste, make haste! One by one the days pass, the auspicious moment may pass before you are ready.'

Madhav replied with folded hands, 'He whose work I do will make haste himself, I am but his instrument.'

The night of the new moon passed. The bright fortnight came round. The blinded Madhav spoke to the stones with his fingers, and the stones spoke to him softly. A guard stood by him, watching, lest he should unbind his eyes.

'The auspicious time for the first *Puja* is on the *ekadasi* night,' the *pundit* came and said, 'Will your work be done by then?'

Madhav bowed and replied, 'Who am I to give an answer? When by the Lord's grace my work is done, I will send you word, if you come before I finish, it will hinder my work and cause delay.'

The sixth day of the moon passed, and the seventh, the moonlight came through the temple windows and fell on Madhav's snow-white hair as he worked.

On the eleventh day, when the sun had set, and the *ekadasi* moon rose in the pale sky, Madhav sighed and said, 'Go, watchman, go and say Madhav's work is done, let not the auspicious moment pass.'

The sentinel left. Madhav unloosed the band that tied his eyes. Through the open door the moonlight fell full upon the image of the god.

Madhav knelt with folded hands, his eyes fixed on his god, tears streamed down his cheeks, the votary had met his god at last,— the pent-up longing of a thousand years shone in his hungry gaze.

The king entered the temple and saw Madhav by the altar with head bent low. One stroke of the king's sword severed Madhav's head,—it was his first adoration, his last obeisance.

July, 1932
Pratham Puja from 'Punashcha'

ETERNITY

*W*hen the desert covering of thousands of years was lifted, there was revealed the mammoth skeleton of a dateless human habitation—which once had life in the invisible void behind the backdrop of History.

Its resonant centuries have consigned all their poetry and song to the depths of an unplumbed silence. And those songs which were still in the germ, in the bud, the immense possibilities that lay latent in the twilight, sank from the unexpressed to the unexpressed.

That too which lay dim behind a veil of smoke, went out. That which sold and that which didn't sell—both went out of the market of this world, imprinted with the same valuation.

Nowhere was left their scar. Nowhere was felt their loss.

Countless aeons have whirled themselves across the serene and silent sky.

Countless new worlds have torn through darkness into the light, and been carried on the eddying foam of countless stars—till, at last, at aeon-end, they have gone the way of the ephemeral insect, of the cloud at the end of the rains.

What an ascetic are you, Eternal Time!
Creations are churned up to the crest of the
waves of your fathomless meditation; are
churned down again to their troughs.

The wheeling dance of the manifest and
the unmanifest gyrates with tremendous
motion, while you stand at its still centre in
unruffled serenity.

O Imperturbable! initiate me into your
ascesis: Place me in the hushed, innermost
recesses of the sacrificial fire of creation, where
reigns an unbroken peace in between life and
death, between attainment and privation.

April, 1935
Anek hazar bacharer maru-jabanikar achchadan . . .
from 'Sesh Saptak'

THE CASUAL

$\mathcal{T}$oday I shall fix no bouquet of flowers in my garden, let there be no coloured thread nor golden tassels.

Folks at home say, 'If you don't tie them round and round, how shall we hold them, how to keep them in the vase?'

I reply: 'Today they are like dancers on holiday, unabashed their laughter: this is their hour of aimless wandering in the afternoon in the *bakula* grove in the fading light of the last month of the year. Today, be content to watch their carefree ways, to listen to their cry, as they sing in snatches. Let that be enough.'

My friend says: 'I came to you thirsting for the full cup, and here like a madcap you tell me, "Today I have shattered the shackles of old familiar form" Why fail in hospitality, old man?'

'Come with me to the fountain,' I reply, 'where the stream glides at its own sweet will, now mighty, now thin. Sometimes it dashes from peak to peak; at others it hides inside a cave. Here and there stand giant stones like rude giants blocking the way. To and fro sway wriggly roots of trees, spreading their fingers like beggars,—in these shining waters what are they looking for?'

The men at the meeting say, 'Ah, this is but your Muse unchained, the captive, where is she?'

'You wont know her today,' I say 'for her seven-ringed necklace gives out no glitter, her pearl-studded bracelets no shine.'

To which they retort, 'Then why all this, in vain? What has she to offer?'

'Only that which one gets from the tree and the flower and the boughs all together', I reply, 'through the leaves the colour filters here and there, in the lashing of the wind you feel its sweet smell, and the open air round, well, it gets just a little heady. That is all.'

'It is not something that you can hold in your grip, you have to see it in its plain dishabille, in its own proper place, in itself, and enjoy it through a mind free from preference.'

1936
Amar phulbaganer phulguli bandhbona aaj torae...
from 'Sesh Saptak'

THE IMPERMANENCE

A traveller am I on the roads of the world. In my wanderings have I seen lands famed in story and shorn of all glory today. I have seen the unheeded ruins of insolent might—its banner of victory is gone with the wind, like boisterous laughter stilled into silence by a sudden thunder-clap.

I have found stupendous pride humbled to the dust, dust on which the beggar spreads his tattered rags, dust on which the traveller leaves the print of weary steps to be effaced by the ceaseless march of unnumbered feet.

I have seen a world long dead lie entombed in layer below layer of sand like some stately ship struck by a sudden storm and sunk in a leaden sea with its cargo of hopes and songs and memories.

Among such symbols of impermanence I move, and feel in the very throbbing of my heart the utter stillness of the infinite.

1936
Pathik ami path chalte chalte dekhechhi . . .
from 'Sesh Saptak'

VAISAKH 25

*C*arrying the stream of many birthdays towards
the final day of death, moves *Vaisakh* the
Twentyfifth.

On that fleeting pedestal sits the Magician,
marks the border of many little lives and deaths
and weaves a garland with many a Rabindranath.

Time moves on its chariot.

The wayfarer en route raises his cup, and gets a
sip of drink; the drink over he falls back into the
dark, and under the wheels his discarded cup
scatters into the dust.

The one who follows and comes with running
feet and a new vessel to wring out a new taste, bears
the same name and is yet perhaps another.

Once I was a boy.

The image that was shaped in the pattern of a
few birthdays, none of you today know what it
was like. Those that knew him are all dead and
gone today.

That boy lives neither in his own self nor in any
one else's memory. He has left for good with his little
world. The echo of his laughter and tears is carried no
more by the wind. Even the broken fragments of his
toys are no longer seen in the dust.

He would sit by life's little window and look at
the beyond. His whole world lay within the limits

190

of that opening. His wide innocent eyes beat against the garden walls, sought to see through the cluster of palm trees. The evenings were thick with fairy tales, with no high fence between faith and unbelief and the mind could easily step from this to the other. In that chiaroscuro of dusk, shadow mingled with substance and belonged to the same order of things.

Those birthdays—they formed an island that basked for a while in the sun and then sank into the ocean of time.

When memory ebbs, one sees now and then its mountain peaks and its crimson shores of coral.

Another age came and brought the call of the twentyfifth day of *Vaisakh* in the early hours of spring in an undefined glow of colour. The young minstrel tuned his lyre and in the mad music of his indefinite sorrow called for the Man of his Heart who lives where no one knows.

Sometimes those strains would reach up to Heaven and move its Mistress. She would in her mercy, at dawn and dusk when the thought of work was all forgotten, send her messengers down the avenues of the *palash* trees, colour drunk and full of shadows. Their soft murmurs have reached my ears, some I have understood, some not. In their dark eyelashes I have seen the hint of tears, on their trembling lips felt the pain of unspoken agony, heard in their ringing bracelets the sudden tingle of eager expectation.

All unknown, they have left for me the fresh flowers of the early morning of the twentyfifth day of *Vaisakh*. My morning dreams thrilled with their heavy fragrance.

That youthful world of birthdays lived side by side with the fairy world in the uncertainty of knowing and not-knowing. There the princess sometimes lay asleep hidden by her own long tresses, and then, touched by the golden wand, she would suddenly stir!

The days passed. The coloured buttresses of purple *Vaisakh* gave way. The path where the shadows trembled to the whisper of the *bakula* forest, where the wind sighed and the midday ached to the wail of the lovelorn cuckoo, where the wings of the butterfly wakened to the invisible call of fragrant flowers, that green and grassy path led me at last to the stone-paved highway.

The youth who had so long practised on his single string now added string on string to his lyre. Then did the twentyfifth day of *Vaisakh* bring me the hard way to the shores of the human sea where waves swelled and roared. I have woven sound on sound at all hours and thrown my net in mid-sea. Some hearts were caught in the net while others slipped and got away.

Sometimes the day has dimmed and despair filled this heart, my mind has stooped with shame. Then in the tired afternoon have come unexpected earthly images from Elysium. They add grace to service, they bring nectar for the tired spirit, they mock fear with the rhythm of their ringing laughter. They awaken the flame of adventure from the fire smouldering in the ashes. Their penance for expression gives form to the message from heaven. They have lighted anew my fading lamp, they have tuned afresh the slack strings of my harp, they have crowned the twentyfifth day of *Vaisakh* with the garland they have woven with their own hands. Their transfiguring touch still lingers in my songs, in my writings.

Then there rang out on life's battlefield the deep notes of conflict and loud opposition. Their echo filled the sky. I had to give up the lyre and take up the trumpet instead. On hot midday, I had to rush through the whirl of success and failure.

Thorns bit into my feet, blood streamed from my wounded breast, stern cruelty dashed my boat to the right and to the left, and sought to drown my life's merchandise in the thick mud of low abuse. Through hatred and affection, jealousy and friendship, music and harsh clamour, through the swell of warm emotions, my world has moved on its path. In the midst of all this hardship, conflict and discontent, you have come to me at this aged hour of the twentyfifth day of *Vaisakh*. Do you know that in what I express, much remains unfulfilled and broken, battered and ignored?

The good and the bad inside and out, the clear and the indistinct, the known and the unknown, all these and the complex mixture of success and failure have helped to shape my image that is reflected today in the mirror of your respect and affection. For him have you brought your garland of love. I accept him as the final form of all my twentyfifth days of *Vaisakhs* and leave for you my blessings. Now that I am about to leave, let this image remain with you. I shall not boast that Time too will keep it so.

When this is done, let me go and be lost in the silent nameless solitude beyond all descriptions woven by the black and white pattern of life. Let me tune my notes with instruments of many melodies and merge in the depths of the primal music.

May, 1936
Panchise Vaisakh from 'Sesh Saptak'

THE COUPLE

*F*rom sunset horizon upsurge colour-rays
ecstatic: The two of them sit before it, side by
side. With all their body and mind—eyes
intent, words silenced, all agitation stilled—
they absorb the message of the sky.

Once they had started on their journey
together—their hearts aflutter with ineffable
joy. Their nuptial bonds were tied with the
living moment as their witness.

Full was that moment and perfect,
unhindered, unconflicting, free from doubt and
fears. Rounded was that moment like a flute
note—infinity converged into an instant. The
narrowest source head was that point of time,
pouring forth in rapture all it had to give, all
its wealth of dance and song, the sunlit
laughter of its gurgling foam.

The stream of those moments is now lost in
the far away where sounds the ocean's chant.
There, in the distance, is the throne set for the
Great One in the spacious court of time.
There, all our joys and all our sorrows mingle
in a mighty union. There, on the canvas of
the sky, the sun limns, rising or setting, its

magic pictures,—with the deepening shadows
of the night brooding over them.

There, sit the two wayfarers silently gazing
at the distant sky. They do not know why
their eyes well up with tears. Deep in their
thought are lodged ideas beyond thought's
language. Is it the premonition of those
unspoken words which moves them so? Have
they begun to see how few are the lines that
tell the trite tale of their love, in the great and
mysterious epic of this vast world?

25 July, 1932
Dujan from 'Beethika'

THE EARTH

*T*oday at the altar of the day's end, as it bows
in a last salutation, I make you my obeisance—
accept it, O Earth!

Valiant are you, meant for heroes only.
Opposites meet in you: at once soft and hard,
you partake of the nature of both man and
woman.
The life of man you sway with an
excruciating conflict. With your right hand
you pour nectar, with your left you break the
chalice,—and fill your playground with
mocking laughter.
A high price you put on what is worth
having, make the heroic life difficult of
attainment, the right to a great life hard to
earn.
No mercy you show to those who ask for it.
Every tree you bear hides the story of battle-
scarred moments, your fruits and crops flaunt
the garlands of your victories.
Over sea and land range your remorseless
battlefields, where death sounds the clarion of
the victory of life. Your ruthlessness is the
foundation on which civilisation builds its
triumphal arch: If there is any lapse, total
destruction is the price thereof.

The demon ruled the beginning of your
history with a might invincible—rough,
savage, insensate.

With mace and club in his fat clumsy
hands, he played havoc with the seas and
mountains, and muddied the skies with a
miasma of fire and gas.

A despot of matter, he had a blind hatred of life.

Then came the gods, who pronounced the
charm that quelled the demon. The insolence
of matter was curbed. The mother of Life
spread her green mantle for her children: On
the orient mount stood the Dawn: Evening
descended with her spell of peace on the
shores of the west.

The shackled demon was brought low: Yet
that primeval savage clings to your history.

Into order he brings a sudden anarchy: Out
of the dark crypts of your nature he wriggles
out all of a sudden: His lunacies still affect the
workings of your pulse.

Day and night the sky, the air, the forests
ring to the exalted chant of the gods, soft and
loud: Yet out of the cavern of your breast that
half-tamed serpent-monster lifts his hood from
moment to moment.

Goaded by him you hurt your own
creatures, ravage your own creations.

Today, at your footstool resting on evil and good, I shall place the obeisance of my scarred life—a homage unto your greatness so terrible and so beautiful.

The massive life, the massive death, secreted in your bowels—today I touch it and feel it all over my body and mind.

The vanished remains of countless men of countless ages are stored in your dust. I too shall leave behind a few handfuls of dust—the residue of all my joys and sorrows:

Leave them behind amid this silent dust-heap that swallows all names, all shapes, all identities.

O fast-bound Earth, Earth free-voyaging amidst the clouds, Earth steeped in the great silence of the mountains, Earth astir with the ceaseless roar of the azure seas, blessed with your fruits, you are beautiful: bereft of them, you are terrible.

Here, your cornfields bowing with ripening harvests—where daily the radiant morning sun wipes out the dewdrops with its mantle of light, and the setting sun leaves its unspoken happiness undulant on the yellowing corn.

There, the devil-dance of mirages in deserts waterless, fruit-less, fear-stricken, skeleton-strewn.

In *Vaisakh* I have seen your storms swoop like a dark hawk on the lightning-pecked horizon; from end to end the sky roars like a

lion puffing its manes; the swish of its tail
sends the mighty forest-tree, its branches in
disarray, grovelling in the dust in despair; the
blown-off roof of a broken hut rushes in the
van of the wind, like an imprisoned bandit
who has broken his chains and makes a bid for
freedom.

Again, in *Phalgun*, I have seen the mild
warmth of your southern breezes strew
soliloquies of union and separation in the scent
of mango-blossoms; while the lunar chalice
brims over with the foam of nectarean wine;
and the sylvan murmur, impatient with the
impertinent wind, bursts into a sudden babble.

Suave you are, you are brutal; old you are,
you are ever new.

In some immemorial dawn you emerged
from the sacrificial fire of a dateless creation;
over your circling ways you have scattered the
remains of hundreds of dilapidated histories, all
meaning spent; have laid, without a twinge of
remorse, your rejected handiworks on layers of
countless oblivions.

Mother of Life, you have kept us in small
cages of fragmented time—within which all
our pastimes must end: all our glories.

It's with no illusions that I have come
before you today; I would not claim from you

any immortality for the garland of days and
nights that I have strung bit by bit all this life.

If I have paid the right price for a seat in a
tiny fragment of those mammoth moments that
emerge and vanish in the course of your multi-
million-year circuit round the sun,

If, with sorrow immeasurable, I have
conquered but one fruitful fraction of life,

Then put on my brow just one earthen
mark of yours—the mark that will fade on the
night when all marks fade into the Great
Unknown.

O heartless Earth, before you forget me
quite, let me place my obeisance today at your
implacable feet.

October, 1935
Aaj amar pranati grahan karo . . .
from 'Patraput'

PEYALI

This wild little plant was given to me, its
leaves yellow-green, its purple flowers like cups
crafted for drinking light.

'What's its name?', I ask. No one knows.

It lives in the world's unknown infinitude
where dwell the nameless stars in the sky.

In a nick-name I bring it captive to my own
little corner of knowing, 'Peyali' is the name.

At the garden's invitation came the dahlia,
the fuchsia, the marigold; this one, in neglected
unmarked freedom remains unbound by caste,
socially unacceptable, a *Baul*.

Before my eyes this flower faded and
drooped. Its tiny sound in the wind never
reached the ear; in the zodiac of its horoscope
the moments that combined are an
infinitesimal sum; the honey that resides in the
depth of its heart is but a minute drop.

In small time is completed its journey, like
an aeon fulfilling the unfolding of the fire-
petalled sun.

Its little history is chronicled in a small
page's corner by the small pen of the universal
recorder.

Side by side the great history is released but
there is no seeing from one page to the next.

The tide of centuries that flows on in slow
timed waves, that stream in which have risen
the mountain ranges and where oceans and
deserts have changed dress, is the same
unceasing time's current whose flow has
furthered the primal resolve of this little flower
through Creation's conflicting forces.

For millions of years in the track of this
flower's blooming and falling that ancient
resolve has remained new, alive, moving, its
final completion not yet visible.

The resolve without form, the picture
without lines is eternal in the Invisible's
contemplation;

The Invisible in whose boundless
imagination I exist, which holds together
man's history of the past, and of Time to come.

October, 1935
Amake ene dilo eai buno charagachti . . .
from 'Patraput'

THIS I

*I*t was from my sentience that the emerald derived its green, and the ruby its red.

I turned my eyes upon the sky and there was light in the East and to the West.

I looked at the rose and said: 'You are beautiful' and the rose gained its beauty.

You may say that this is metaphysics and not poetry. My answer is that it is the Truth and therefore poesy.

You may call it my vanity but it is so on behalf of all men. It is on the canvas of man's vanity that the creator displays his art of creation.

With every breath inhaled or exhaled the ascetic strives for negation: for him no emerald, no ruby, no light, no rose, neither you nor I.

On the other hand, He who is beyond all limits is seeking by His own will to achieve the limit of man, and it is Him we call I.

There was a confluence of darkness and light in the assertion of that Ego, and shape appeared and emotions found form.

As if by magic, negation became a yes, in colour and form, in sorrow and joy.

Do not call this mere metaphysics.

My mind is full of joy as I sit in the creative

court of the cosmic —I, with brush in hand
and bowls of paint.

The learned say: The ancient moon with its
heartless and cynical smile creeps closer to the
ribs of the world like a messenger of death.

Some day it will heave a vast tug to the
oceans and hills and this world of matter and
form will give place to an Amorphous Void,
that will swallow all debits and credits of days
and nights.

Human action will lose even the pretence
of immortality, and his puny history will be
swallowed in the blackness of eternal night.

I say that Man's departing eyes will wrench
the very colour from day, his fading mind will
draw away the throb of all emotions.

Vibrant energy may still walk from sky to
sky, but nowhere will there be Light.

The musicians will make empty gestures, but
there will be neither instruments nor music.

Bereft of poetry the Maker, engaged in the
calculations of existence devoid of personality,
will sit, desolate and alone, in a sky devoid of
all colour.

Nowhere in this universe, not in its farthest
reaches, not in spaces beyond eternity's sway
in worlds upon worlds, will these words

resound, 'You are beautiful', and 'I love.'

Will the Maker then, once again, sit in meditation age upon age, and chant in prayer 'Speak, speak, speak again, say... "You are beautiful". Repeat ... "I love".'

May, 1937
Ami from 'Shyamali'

206

THE CARESS

*E*very day I call you by your known name,
call you Charu; but suddenly it occurred to me
that I would like to call you in some other
way, in a form of caress, in more simple words,
by a name universal in manner and meaning
. . . My love.

I have called you that quietly in the privacy
of my thoughts, and heard in answer your loud
laughter. I expect it is understandable, for these
are not days for soft sweet laughter; Ujjain and
Avanti are no more, the classical age is over.

You ask what is wrong with your work-a-
day name. I shall tell you. I had returned early
from work and lolled on the back porch, feet
hooked to rails, the evening paper in my
hands. Suddenly I looked into the ante-room
and there you were dressing for the evening.

You were pleating your hair before the
mirror and sticking pins and combs in your
dark tresses. It was ages since I had watched
you so closely, watched you arch your neck
and bend your head as you deftly coiled and
built up the twisted braids of hair. It was a long
time since I had heard the whispered clink of
bangles as your two hands moved in unison.

207

Finally you wrapped round yourself a scarlet cloth, tucked it here, loosened it there, draped lower in one place, and in another pulled up, like a poet changing the rhythm by altering the shape of lines and words.

Today I realised for the first time how the housewife pays back in coins of beauty and love for the small earnings brought by us, pedestrian wage-earners.

I looked at you and it was not the work-a-day Charu. In this very manner, in another age, did *Avantika* show herself decked in love's beauty to the eyes of love. Charu also would have fitted in the metrical verse of a deathless century. She comes as in a tryst from her boudoir to the living room: She comes like a vision from far off ages to the world of today.

I walked out into the garden, and decided that I too will add prestige to my feelings by decorating it with a work of art: when I next call you to me, it will be a declaration of love.

I saw in front the creeper covered with white blossom. I can never recall its foreign name and call it star-dust instead, for its scent fills the night like a babble of flowers.

This year it has blossomed out of season as if it could not wait for winter to end. I plucked

a bunch of flowers—they too will add their
signature to my scroll.

In this quiet twilight you are Charuprabha
of the classic tales, and I your Ajit Kumar.

I have just a few words to say to you today,
words laid out as a gesture of love, built up by
my fancy as you have done your hair with its
coils and twists.

If you must, do laugh, but I shall still have
my say, 'Beloved, these bunches of alien
flowers were longing for the dark sky of the
springtime night, I have brought them to you
that they may find rest in your ink-black hair.'

30 May, 1936
Sambhashan from 'Shyamali'

A SENSE OF BEING

*L*et me listen, I wait to hear. The hour is late, and at this ending of the day, the birds pour out in spendthrift abandon all the sweetness of their song. They are drawing me, mind and body, into the very heart of melody and colour, into a mansion rich with the play of life.

The record of their history has no message save this: We are, we are alive, we are quick with life in this magic moment, this astonishing Present.

The message reached my inmost heart. Like girls who fill their pots at the village pool at dusk, I immerse my mind in this welter of sound in the sky and fill it to the brim.

Give me a little time, I have outspread my mind, I wait.

In this ebb-tide hour the evening light is spread upon the grass, and the trees are full of silent joy, joy that is hidden in the marrow of bones, joy that is strewn among the leaves.

My heart blends itself into this breeze and feels the caress of the universal breath transmuted by my consciousness.

Do let me sit and rest awhile, to dream with eyes wide open.

You have come with your disputations but today at day's end, at this sunset hour, I find myself possessed of no time for them.

There is for me at this magic hour neither right nor wrong, neither praise nor blame, neither conflicts nor hesitations.

There is only the forest green and the shimmer of water, a mild tremor in the flow of living, a brief clamour, the agitation of a wave.

This momentary pause that belongs to me is flying across the western sky, like a moth that spreads its iridescent wings to end at sunset its brief-lived day. Do not ask me questions, they are profitless.

What will it serve to bring me your demands? From this present my gaze is turned away, I rest on a sand-bar that slopes towards the past.

The time is gone, when my aching heart wandered in the light and shade woven by leaves and branches.

The soliloquy of the wind across the fields and in the flowering sedge as it moved over the shimmering grass under the noon-tide beams of a September day mingled with the pauses of my song.

The web of questions that entangled life in its toils is gone. The pilgrim on the fated road has left behind no endeavour, no anxiety, no desire.

Only in the murmur of the leaves is left a memory, they also lived: a greater truth this than that they are no more.

Today we sense the throb of colour in their clothes, the breath of their movement, the message of clinging eyes, the rhythm of love.

Into the day's white river of faith flows in westward movement the dark blue river of love.

1 June, 1936
Praner Rash from 'Shyamali'

AFRICA

*I*n those restless early days when dissatisfied
with himself, the Creator tossed his head and
destroyed again and again his own creations in
impatient gestures.

O Africa, the rude arms of the ocean
snatched you away from the bosom of your
mother East and imprisoned you under the
close watch of the forest trees in the inmost
court of darkness.

There in the long hours of solitary leisure
you looked for the mystery of the inaccessible,
sought to understand the difficult hints of sky
and water.

The supernatural awoke in you a magic
chant beyond the bounds of consciousness.

You mocked terror in the guise of the
terrible, you sought to defeat fear by building
yourself an aura of awe that echoed to the
thunder of your drums.

O veiled one, the clouded vision of the eyes
of disdain could not recognise your humanity
under the dark shadows.

Iron handcuffs in their hands, came hordes
with claws sharper than the wolves, came
human butchers whose blind pride was darker
than your sunless forests.

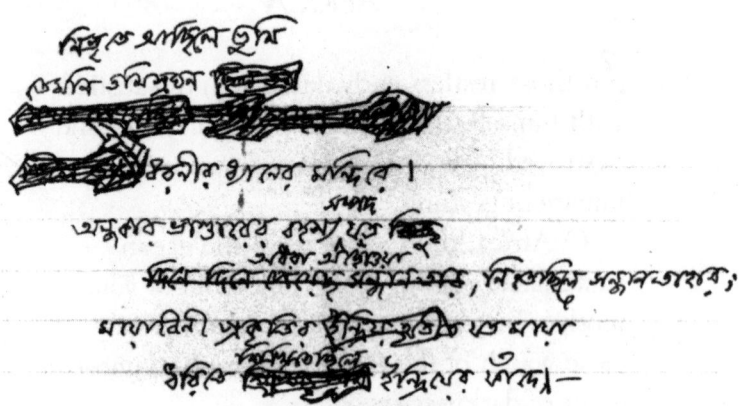

বিতৃষ্ণ মানুষের তুমি
তেমনি চিরসুন্দর

ফুটনীর থালের মন্দিরে।

অনুকথ ভাবনাবের সুদূর পথে

মিলে মিলে , নির্জনুবুর সন্ধ্যাবেলায়;
মায়াবিনী সুব্রতার ই দুই গ্রা মায়া

হুরিত ইন্দ্রিয়ের সাঁঝ—

সুন্দর হে আদিম,
কালো এরন্টগুঠের জল

এমন সমরবিতের ক্ষ সুপ্তিরঙ্গলনীর ক্ষণতু—
রূপমদোদ্ধত ইন্দুমতী,
সুন্দরেশ সিংহজিল দীপ-হীন কোমল সুন্দরে,—

তোমার হঙ্কর পাবে ধলমধেন্তু বম,

যেমন কথামভরা মানব হৃদয়
তরঙ্গায়ে তিল সুসায়িত,
মাতের চুরু লেন্ডে নন্দ সবিতির এতুকাবে

নিঃস্বঙ্গ অসস্তৃষিতা।
এস্তু ও ব রুক্ত সাথে মিশে

ভারতীর ক্ষণ্বের পথ
দ্বিধুক্ত মাদিল কবি—

The savage greed of the civilised came out
in naked inhumanity. The forest paths were
misty with sighs, their dust was clotted with
your blood and tears.

The trampled earth beneath the nailed
shoes of the bandits left their everlasting mark
on your tragic history.

All the while in their temples the bells rang
morning and evening in the name of God the
merciful.

Children played, and poets sang in the
worship of beauty.

Today, when on the Western horizon
Evening stands stifled by storms, when beasts
emerge from cavernous depths to announce
the end of light in ugly shrieks,

O Poet of an epoch's end, come and stand
before the humiliated woman in the glow of
the impending gloom, ask for her forgiveness.

Let this be your last sacred word of faith in
this cacophony of cruel hatred.

February, 1937
Africa from 'Patraput'

A STRANGE DREAM

*O*ne night I dreamt a strange dream; Binu
was calling to me, 'Wake up and see what is
happening.'

I sat up and saw Calcutta shuffling along
with uncertain steps as thousands of beams and
rafters knocked against one another. The brick
built houses marched ahead like rhinos while
doors and windows banged and clanged. The
streets moved like huge pythons and on their
back clattered trams and carriages. The shops
and markets bobbed up and down while roofs
hit one another on the head in a drunken
orgy. The Howrah bridge crawled like a giant
scorpion and Harrison Road trailed behind.
The Monument reeled, as if a mad elephant
was waving its trunk in the air. Our school was
rushing forward madly, with arithmetic and
grammar books running fast. The maps were
fluttering on the wall like birds flapping their
wings. The bells tolled ceaselessly and without
break with no heed of the hour.

Millions cried, 'Stop this madness, for where
is it you want to go and whence?'

Drunken with movement, Calcutta paid no
heed, for the lure of dance had made even
pillars and walls restless.

I thought to myself 'what does it matter if
Calcutta goes straight to Bombay? If she prefers

Delhi, Lahore or Agra, all we need do is to put a turban on her head and horned shoes on her feet. Or if she wants to rush off to England, all the people will become hatted coated and booted Englishmen!'

Suddenly there was a bang and I woke. Calcutta was as always still in Calcutta.

January, 1930
Ekadash Path from 'Shahaj Path, Part II'

THE BEACON

*T*here is a lone girl on the darkening beach
who looks at the sky and floats her lighted
lamp on the water.

She knows that her mother has gone to
heaven and is hopeful that she will return by
the ferry provided by the lamp.

The world swarms with millions, the roads
that cross the earth are numberless, many are
the countries that remain unknown and
strange mountains raise their heads: in the
midst of this multiplicity can the mother see
from heaven the tiny nook where the two of
them—brother and sister—live?

Does their mother go seeking for them in
the darkness and lose her way again and again
among the clustered stars in the infinite void?

The daughter's hand has lit a lamp and will
keep it burning so that the mother may
recognise the light from across the far off
spaces.

In their sleep, will the mother come to their
motherless bed and kiss them goodnight night
after night?

July, 1937
Akash Pradeep from 'Chharar Chhabi'

FAREWELL

*I*t is time for the bird to leave. Soon the forest winds shall scatter to the ground the nest bereft, shaken and songless.

With the dried leaves and flowers, I shall be swept away at the day's end to the pathless wastes of space beyond the setting sun.

For ages this friendly earth has been my home. I have heard the call of spring full of gracious gifts and sweet with mango buds. The *Ashoka* blooms have yearned for my songs and I have filled them with my love. Sometime *Vaisakh* storms have raged, the warm dust has choked my voice and crippled my wings.

Blessed am I in all this. Life's honour has been mine.

When my tired journey here will be over, I shall look back once and leave an humble salute as my last homage to the Lord of Life.

April, 1934
Jabar samay holo bihanger... from 'Prantik'

THE END

*W*hen the lights on the stage went out one
by one, and the theatre was emptied of
audience, my mind sank to quiet at the
beckoning of silence, like a sleep whose dream-
pictures are inked out in the darkness.

The make-up that I had fashioned so long
for my stage-appearance since the curtain went
up, came to nothing in a moment.

To present myself to the multitude I had
decked myself in a variety of colours and
insignia: all these were wiped out.

The depth of my fullness in myself reduced
me to a wondering silence like that of the
clear sky hushed in star-lit self-realisation when
the variegated make-up of the earth fades into
the blank of the day's end that witnesses the
funeral of the sun.

9 October, 1937
Rangamanche ake ake nibe gelo jabe deepsikha . . .
from 'Prantik'

INVOCATION

*I*n the tired twilight of consciousness, I saw this body floating adown the dark stream of oblivion, carrying away all sensations, all its strange sorrows, all its accumulations of memory clothed in a many hued envelop, all its music embodied in the flute.

As I move farther and farther away, the impressions fade: the sound of vesper along familiar coasts by the tree-encircled villages grows faint; the doors close, the light is dimmed, the boats lie at anchor in a lonely landing place.

The river traffic comes to a halt. The night thickens. On the forest boughs the muted bird-song offers its sacrifice at the feet of the Great Silence.

A dark Formlessness descends upon the world's rich diversity on land and water. My body fades into a shadow, a mere point that disappears into the infinite Night.

Standing alone, at the altar of the stars, I look upward and with hands upraised cry:

O sole seer, O illumining Sun, Thou hast withdrawn thy rays but reveal again thy light, the Lustre that is thy most blessed form. Let me behold in Thee the self that is the same in thee and me.

8 December, 1937
Dekhilam abasanna chetanar godhulibelay . . . from 'Prantik'

HISSING SERPENTS

*H*issing serpents poison the very air.
    Here fine words of peace ring hollow.
    My time is up; but before I go, I send out
my call to those who are getting ready in a
thousand homes to fight the demon.

25 December, 1937
Naginira charidike pheliteche bishakta nishwas . . .
from 'Prantik'

222

SHYAMA

*F*airish dark complexion, chain of coral beads
about her neck—I looked upon her in
amazement, and she, at the threshold of youth,
gazed unabashed from big mascaraed eyes.

My age was almost hers.

The picture comes to me clearly: the south
door half open, and in the morning sunlight
the almond tree's top branches thick with
shiny leaves, newly opened to the faint blue
sky.

On her girlish body a white sari—the black
border encircled her and fell in the circles
round her feet—two golden bangles on her
rounded wrists; I had seen that figure in the
pages of a story book some lazy afternoon; from
time to time she had beckoned me to a
mirage-world far away at the edge of a body's
dreams, where many idle fancies roamed.

The magic of her body threw unseen
shadows on my mind and body, so subtle yet
so tangible. I did not dare to speak to her. An
inexpressibly soft murmur of pain went through
my heart—she was far away, so far away: as far
as the topmost *shireesh** branches, down from
which gently, gently falls a faint perfume to the
depths of one's being.

---

* *Shireesh* is a large flowering tree with pale green or light pink flowers having a sweet but
very faint odour.

One day she left a note—an invitation to her dolls' wedding. Her guests were all playing and laughing and talking. A shy boy, I sat in a corner oppressed by my own timidity.

The evening passed in vain. I have no memory of what dishes I was served. My eyes were on her feet as she flitted about with quick steps, and the black border of her sari danced around them.

From the corner of my eyes I saw the bright sunshine captured in the golden bangles round her wrists. I listened to her soft cool voice, requesting, insisting: back in my room I heard their echoes half the night.

After that, one day no barriers remained. One day I called her by her pet name. One day all fears vanished.

Freely we talked, with banter and many a joke. Sometimes an imagined fault was followed by pretended anger; sometimes cruel fun with mocking words caused pain, sometimes one blamed the other for indifference.

And sometimes I have seen her negligently dressed—busy with her cooking pots and quite unabashed. My masculine blunders she rebuked with the sharp pride of her feminine wit.

One day she said: 'I can read your palm.' She took my hand within her hand, bending low, examining the lines.

She said: 'Your nature is weak in signs of love.' I made no reply. The true reward of touch effaced the false accusation.

But there remained the pain of not knowing her. Beauty is always distant—even when close, you only feel eternal non-attainment.

Chequered days of joy and sadness, one beyond the other, dissolve in the western horizon. The blue of the *Chaitra** sky deepens its loveliness. The light of *Asvin** plays the festive *shanai*** in the golden paddy fields. Slowly sails the dream-filled boat, who knows in what direction.

31 October, 1938
Shyama from 'Akash Pradeep'

---

*   *Chaitra* and *Asvin* are Bengali months, the first from mid-March to mid-April, and the second from mid-September to mid-October.
** *Shanai* is a wind instrument resembling an oboe but larger and with a sharper, more powerful tone, associated with wedding and festivals.

একদিন তরীখানা আমাদের যেখানে এই ঘাটে লেগে,
বসন্তের সকল হাওয়ায় বেগে।
তোমরা সবাই দাঁড়াইলে মোর ডাকি
কাহারে কোনো আর না কি ?
যাহা কেহ আনে?
তবুও শুধু চলেছি, কে জানে?

নদীতে লাগিল দোলা, দাঁড়ের পড়িল টান,
দূর হতে লাগিলাম যৌবনের বেদনা গান।
সেই গানখানি
কুসুমিত তরুতলে তরুণ তরুণী,
তুলিল অলক,
মোর সাথে দিয়ে তারা কহিল, এ আমাদেরই লোক।
আর কিছু নয়,
সে মোর প্রথম পরিচয়।

তার পরে কতবার বেলা
সাঁঝে হোলো, সাঁঝে হোলো ভোরাইর মেলা,
মোদিনের ক্ষুধা সমা
বিস্মৃত দিনের কথা সকলের ধার ধার;

THE INTRODUCTION

*O*nce my boat, moved by the fresh winds of early spring, stopped at this landing place. You had all crowded round and asked, 'Who are you and where do you go?'

The river swelled, the boat tugged at the ropes. I sat alone and sang about the pangs of youth. Young lovers beneath flowering trees heard my song, plucked the *Ashoka* bloom and offered it as a gift, saying, 'He is one of us.' This alone was my first introduction.

The flood tide ended, the waves no longer rippled and laughed. The languid song of the cuckoo suddenly brought back to mind the memory of forgotten days. The golden *champak* drooped and was carried far away. Torn shreds from the gay invitation of festival nights in early spring, they were now meaningless.

The ebb-tide strongly pulled the boat towards the far-off sea. Boys and girls, young travellers of a new age, looked at me from a distance and asked, 'Who is it that sails in his boat towards the setting sun?'

I tuned my harp and sang once again, 'Let my only description be that I am one of you. Let this and nothing else be my final introduction.'

January, 1937
Parichaya from 'Senjuti'

THE STATION

*M*ornings and evenings to the railroad
station I come. I like to watch the crowd
hurrying to get their tickets. To up trains, to
down trains they rush and go away, and some
miss their trains because of a last minute lapse.

> Rattle, rattle, all the day,
> A storm of crowded coaches,
> Changing motion, swing and sway,
> Now east, now west approaches.

This scene, like a motion-picture, makes me
think of endless meetings and forgettings of
ceaseless welcomes and farewells. Crowds
gather every minute upon the stage, they wave
their flags and disappear leaving no address.
And behind all this is the strong pull of
pleasure and of grief, of gain, and things gone
wrong.

> Round the clock, the signals cluster,
> Round the clock, the whistles bleat,
> Hurry, hurry, jostle, fluster,
> Some leave, and some are late.

Of all this going and staying behind
nothing remains except a series of images.
They catch the eye for a moment and then

228

vanish. It's all a game of self-derision; over, as soon as begun. Bits of battered canvas fall in heaps by the roadside and are blown away by the weary breeze of summer. Those who sob at partings themselves, a minute later, rush away with their tears scarcely dry.

> Dong! Dong! sounds the bell,
> Windows crammed with faces,
> Comes the moment of farewell,
> A twinkle all effaces.

Thus I realise that this world is the work of an artist, not a blacksmith's hammered product; meant for the eyes, but not for the hand to clutch. Throughout the rise and fall of the ages, throughout all comings and goings the series is never broken, never lost are the pictures. And with this continuous passing show, all by myself, I remain at the railroad station.

> One brush the pictures makes anew,
> Another blacks them out,
> Here's a throng has just pushed through,
> There's another put to rout.

7 July, 1938
Ishteshan from 'Naba Jatak'

THE NIGHT EXPRESS

*T*his heart of mine, a night express, is on the way. The night is deep, the carriages are loaded all with sleep.

What seems a murky nothing plunged in the infinite dark, awaits the frontiers of sleep in lands unspecified.

Moments aglow in flashes are instantly left behind. Unknown territories, addresses invisible whirl through the speechless night towards the unthinkable, endless far away, the final destination.

The driver's name is not announced. Some say it's a mere machine, call it mindless, and yet surrender themselves to its blindness. They feel, as they make their beds, that this uncertain thing would arrive unfailing at a certainty. Behind the screen a doubt there gleams a veiled assurance, a breath is wafted from the people hidden in those nameless tracts which are crossed time after time.

The train rolls on, under the sky not a moment's rest; unconscious, folded in slumber, there's just a hope of a distant dawn.

28 March, 1940
Rater Gadi from 'Naba Jatak'

ALL THAT REMAINS

The grace of your right hand's touch you
denied me.
    On the courtyard of my thoughts your light
and shadows come and go composing—then
rubbing out—an *alipan*.*

    In the month of *Vaisakh* the emaciated river
withheld from me the favour of a full stream.
    The hesitant shallow current only awoke
the thirsty mind at the bank's edge.

    Whatever little I received in the cupped
palms of my timid desires may not fill them to
overflowing.
    Still, I've collected something after a whole
day's emptiness—store enough for a lifetime's
dream.

30 September, 1939
Udbritta from 'Sanai'

---

* *alipan* or *alpana*: design in earth colours executed on the floor by women of a household on
ceremonial occasions.

OCTOBER, 1938

Fuslee.—Kartik, 1346.   Mus.—Shaban, 1357.
Samvat.—Kartik, (Sudee), 1995.   Beng.—Kartik, 1345.

25 Tuesday [298—67]

Mus.—16 Kartik.   Sam.—2 Kartik (Sudee).   Mus.—30 Shaban.
Beng.—8 Kartik, Bhratri Dwitiya, 2-27 d.

বসেছিলে তুমি আসন পাতি

জানালার পাশে —   মধুপুর পথ দিয়ে

          ছড়ায়ে দিলো।

কলতান   চারিধার   জুড়ে দিলো।

তোমার সে উদাসীনতা

          সত্য কিনা জানিনাসে

চোখে চরম সোনা ঘাসে ঘাসে

          বেদনা মেলে।

          সুরভয় পাতায়

          বিন্দু বিন্দু রবেমূল

শ্যামল বিমুল ভূমি

          করে স্তূপ তুল।

তুমি চলে গেলে ধীরে ধীরে

          সুখস্মৃতির

পিছনে নীপ দীর্ঘিকায়

          তৃষার্ত মেলো।

OF TWO MINDS

*Y*ou came—but all the same you did not come. At least that's what you meant to tell me by your truant footsteps flung upon the path before my room.

Did your indifference reveal to me in mockery my emptiness? And was that indifference assumed? I do not know. Did they, your running footsteps, really unfurl that neglect on the grass?

Drops of rain fall on the leaves, water is shining under the trees in the grove.
Far away in the leafy shadows you seem to have dissolved in the rain-loud enchantment, and left behind the game of sun and shadow which you played.

January, 1940
Duvidha from 'Sanai'

তোমার চরিত্রে আমি করিনা বিশ্বাস।

যদি কোন কিছু আর

নিয়ে কভু যাব

দিনে দিনে দিব মুখ করি।

তোমার বিমুখে আপনারে।

দুই বেলা এই   পায়ে ভাই

। এ হিয়ের নিত্যসুখ

         সুখস্বপ্নে দীন করে নাই

আমি জানি এর ধার সংসারের

রস তুমি কর চুরি

সন্ধ্যা দিবে স্মরণ করিতে অধুর

এ বিশ্বে ভালবাসিয়াছি।

এ ভালবাসি রস, এ গ্লেনের

বিদায় নেবার কালে   দান।

এ সকল আমার এ

। এ অধীকার।

NOT MY ACHIEVEMENT

*I*t's not my achievement that I trust. I know
the constant waves of time will break upon it
day by day and obliterate it.

My faith is in myself; this cup I have filled
with the universe and drunk. And filled it too
with every moment's love.

The weight of sorrow made no crack, its art
was blackened by no dust.

When I finally leave the stage, I know the
flowering grove will season after season bear
witness that I loved this world.

A lifetime's gift, this love is the truth. At
the time of my departure this truth, unfading,
will deny death.

28 November, 1940
Amar kirtire ami korina biswas . . .
from 'Rog Shajya'

শ্রীবিবেকের খানিক রাতে সুবোধিন্দু বরে

শ্রী বিমল্য মাবে আস্ত রাগে—

লক্ষ কোটি নক্ষত্র

এমনু বিবরের মেঘা বিকশে তোদের রুমারীরা

চুবেছে সাবিত্রীরা মিরকের শুনতে প্রশিয়া

দিকে দিকে,

তোমার অন্তহীন সেই আকাশের বক্ষমূলে

একসময় করেছি উত্থান

তোমার রাজের পাত মাধুর্ষ সুবলিষ্ঠের মতো

শরীরবাহী কতদ্বীর ইতিহাস।

এসেছি সে পৃথিবীতে

যেথা রক্তের রক্তের দীঠি

প্রালয়ঙ্কী সমুদ্রের গর্ভ হতে উঠি

দুর্ত্ত বিহাট একতারে

ঈশ্বরাখিল আকাশের ঠীরে অর্কাশ আঠংঠ

কাছে রূপনুরে।

সগিরুর

এসমুর্ষ শ্রী মাতনরীথ সুরঙরে চুরা

আমরু রাষ্ট্র ছিল খসু লোক দীর্ঘ সুখ দীবা।

ON MY BIRTH DAY

*A*s I step into the eightieth year of my life, my
mind wakes to this wonder today:

In the silent flood of light of the fiery
stream of a billion stars that sweep at
unimaginable speed through the soundless
Void, I have suddenly arisen in the linked
history of centuries like an instant's spark in
the festival of eternal creation underneath that
sky, dark and limitless.

I have come to a world where aeon after
aeon life's plasma rose from the womb of the
sea and revealed its secret and splendid
identity as it spread its branches in many a
changing guise in the immense abyss of matter.

The drowsy shadows of an imperfect
twilight existence had brooded over the animal
world for ages, waiting anxiously—for whom?

At the end of countless days and nights
man appeared on the stage of life with slow
heavy steps. New lamps were lit one after the
other, new values found form and voice; in an
ethereal glow man saw the image of his
splendid future.

On the world's stage is seen in act after act
the slow unfolding of consciousness.

I too have dressed for my part among the actors in the drama. To my delighted wonder, I too have been called to discover the stage.

This world of life, this earthly dwelling of the soul with its sky and light and wind, its earth, sea and mountain hides a deep purpose and wheels round the sun.

Bound to that mystery, I came eighty years ago and shall depart in a few years time.

May, 1940
Jibaner ashi barshe prabeshinu jabe . . .
from 'Janmadine'

ASSURANCE

*W*hen I do not see you, in sick imagination I think the earth under my feet is conspiring to move away.

And I lift my arms in anxiety to clutch at the empty sky.

I wake with a start and at once see you are still there beside me: sitting with bent head, knitting wool, with a look of invincible peace about you.

5 December, 1940
Tomare dekhina jabe . . .
from 'Rog Shajya'

THE POET OF MAN

*H*ow little I knew of this great big world.

Of towns and cities in diverse lands, of man's varied deeds, of rivers and seas, deserts and mountains, of strange animals and unfamiliar trees—so much has remained beyond my ken.

Amid the world's immensity, my mind occupies but a tiny corner. Stung by this awareness, I collect with ceaseless ardour words and images from tales of travel, and try to fill up the store of my meagre knowledge with riches I have begged from others.

I am a poet of the earth. I strive that all its sounds shall seek expression in my flute, and yet there are many gaps. Many notes have failed to find their way to this music making.

The earth's great orchestra has often in silent moments filled my life through images and hints.

The unheard song that inaccessible snowy mountains sing to the silent blue of the heavens has again and again moved my heart. The unknown star over the South Pole that keeps its long vigil in utter loneliness has at midnight hours touched my sleepless eyes with ineffable light. The violent, surging waterfall has sent from afar its voice to the depth of my mind.

Poets from many lands pour their songs into Nature's symphonic stream. I have this link with all of them: I enjoy their company, partake of their joy, receive the blessing of the Muse and a taste of the music of the universe.

Most inaccessible of all is man, hidden behind his own self, and with no measure in time and space. He has an inner life that is revealed only through a communion of minds. Barred by the fences I have raised, I do not always find an entry into that secret world.

The peasant tills the field, the weaver works his loom, the fisherman casts his net—their varied work extends far and wide and the world moves on their support.

I live in a small corner in the perpetual exile of prestige, seated by a narrow window on society's high platform. Sometimes I have ventured near their homes but have lacked the courage to enter.

Without a meeting of lives the store of songs can collect only false merchandise. So I accept blame and admit the incompleteness of my tunes. I know that my poetry, though it has wandered on many paths, has yet not found its way everywhere.

I wait for the message of the poet who is close to the soil, who shares the peasant's life and becomes his kin through word and action.

For ever do I look for what I myself cannot give to poetry's joyful feast. But let the gift be real and not tempt the eye by appearance. It is not good to steal a literary badge, to acquire a name without paying the price. False, false is such fashionable love for the labourer.

Come, poet of mute, obscure men, give voice to their hidden sorrow, fill with life and joy this dry, songless land, release the spring hidden in its heart.

Let there be honour also for those who in the court of the Muse play one-stringed harps in the orchestra. Let us listen to those who are wordless in sorrow and joy, who stand silent and humble before the world, who live near us and yet remain unknown.

If you be their kin, let your renown make them known! I shall offer you salutations again and again.

21 January, 1941
Bipula e prithivir katatuku jani . . .
from 'Janmadine'

THE COSMIC STAGE

*O*n the vast stage of the cosmos, Pyrotechnics of suns and stars flash from sky to sky, from aeon to aeon-end.

I too have come carrying a particle of fire from the unseen and unbegun to one small corner of a narrow strip of space and time.

Today as I reach the final act the lights begin to dim, and in the gathering shadows is betrayed the illusory nature of this play. The stage-costumes of joy and sorrow start slipping off slowly; and I see lying outside the theatre-door heaps of multi-coloured garments discarded by millions of actors and actresses from age to age.

As I look beyond, far in the background I discern the *Nataraja*, the Master of the Revels, solitary and silent behind hundreds of extinguished stars.

3 February, 1941
Virat srishtir khetre atasbajir khela akashe akashe . . .
from 'Arogya'

সৃষ্টি লীলার সুধাদনের সুধার দাঁড়াইছে

দেখি আলে সুর্ষ

তমসের পর পার,

যেথা মহ্য অব্যুজের   তৈরত্যে বিভু শীল।

আজি এ সুপ্রভাত কালে   কহে মোর মনে

হেরো কোরো অসুরভূত হেমুর্ষ আলোস আবরুন,

তোমার অনুভ্ত্তম   বোধির মাঝ্য দিষি

আপনার অন্তরার সুকৃষ্ণ।

যে আমি দিনের   বায়ুতে মিশায় প্রানবায়ু,

তব্ম   পার দেহ হৃদ

দ্যা কহ্য   সে আসন না দেমুক

মত্ত্যর বীর্য্যা কৃপাবেশ।

এ মর্ত্ত্যের নীলাক্ষেত্রে সুখ দুখে অমৃতের জ্ম

দেখেছি তো   দিন ফলে,

তুমি যাচ্ছি এ দ্বোর লক্ষ পণ্ঠ স্থির লইয়াছি   তবে বার অমীমের দেখেছি শ্রীমার অনুরাগে
সেই সুরুডের কলে,   খেলা
সে সংগীত অনির্বচনীয়।   আমীর দেয়ালার বেশে   সুর্ষের

                 দিয়ে যার জীবনের

                                   সুন্দরের মৃত্যুর গীতা।

১২ মাঘ
১৩৪৭

THE FINAL OFFERING

*A*t the far end of the stage of the world's play I
stand. Each moment do I see the shore beyond
the darkness where in the vast consciousness of
the Unmanifest I once lay merged.

On this morning spring to my mind the words
of the seer, 'Lift, lift thy veil of light, O Sun, that
in thy inmost core of radiance I may behold my
own true Self.'
The 'I' whose breath of life at the end of day is
one with the air, whose body ends in ashes—may
that 'I' not cast its shadow on the path disguised
as Truth.

In the playhouse of the world, many a time
and oft have I tasted immortality in sorrow and in
joy. Again and again have I seen the Infinite
through the veil of the limited. For me the final
meaning of life lay there: In beauty's forms, in
harmonies divine.

Today, when the door of the playhouse opens I
shall make my final bow, and leave behind in the
temple of the earth my offerings of a life-time that
no death can touch.

January, 1941
Srishti lilapranganer prante danraiya dekhi khone khone . . .
from 'Janmadine'

THEY WORK

*L*azily, floating on time's stream my mind
gazes into infinity. And traversing through
space I see myriad pictures drawn in light and
shade.

Aeon on aeon, in the lengthening past
have marched masses of men proudly, with
victory's arrogant speed.

Here came Pathans, empire-hungry, and
then the Mughals, waving storms of dust and
flags of triumph.

I look, today, into the alleys of space. They
have vanished without a trace, but from age to
age sunrise and sunset have reddened the
speckless blue.

Again, under that sky, have come marching
columns of the mighty British, along iron-
bound roads and in chariots spouting fire,
scattering the flames of their force.

I know that the flow of time will sweep
away their empire's enveloping nets, and the
armies, bearers of its burden, will leave not a
trace in the path of the stars.

I turn my eyes on this earth, our earth, and
see multitudes moving with vibrant voices
along many roads and in many groups, from
age to age, working to meet daily needs of men
who live and die.

Through eternity they pull the oars, hold
the helm. In field after field, they sow and cut
the corn. They work in town and country.

Royal sceptres break, War-drums cease,
Victory towers gape, stupidly, self-forgetful.
Bloodstained arms and blood-shot eyes are
lost in children's tales.

The people work. In every country, go
where you will. In Anga, in Banga, in
Kalinga's seas and river-*ghats*, in Punjab,
Bombay, and Gujrat.
The hum and the roar of their toil link
nights and days, made vibrant by work.
Sorrows and joys, from day to day, orchestrate
life's great music.
Empires by the hundred collapse and on their
ruins the people work.

13 February, 1941
Alas samaydhara beye mon chale shunya pane cheye...
from 'Arogya'

247

SALUTATION

*S*weet is this globe, sweet the dust of the
earth: this is the great refrain, this the message
of a fulfilled life that I have accepted in my
heart.

The gifts of truth which came to me day
after day are all sweet and shall never wither.

On death's frontier the song wells up in my
heart: imperfections fade and the bliss of the
infinite endures.

When I shall feel the touch of the earth for
the last time, I shall at parting say,

'I have anointed my forehead with thy dust,
seen the glow of the eternal behind the
shadows of adversity.'

'Earth embodies the truth in the form of
bliss—because I have known this, I salute the
dust.'

14 February, 1941
E dyulok madhumaya, madhumaya prithibir dhuli . . .
from 'Arogya'

ON THE BANKS OF THE RUPNARAYAN

I woke up on the banks of the Rupnarayan.
    I knew for certain this world is not a dream.
I saw my own form writ in letters of blood. I
recognised myself through shock and blow,
through pain and suffering.
    Truth is stark and strong, I loved its
ruggedness—it never deceives.
    Life is a pilgrimage of sorrow till the very
end: an endeavour to win the ultimate value
of truth, to pay back all debts in final death.

13 May, 1941
Rupnarayaner kule jege uthilam . . .
from 'Sesh Lekha'

THE UNANSWERED QUESTION

Faced with the emergence of new Being, the first day's sun asked the question: 'Who art thou?'

There was no reply.

Endless years passed.
On the shores of the western sea, in the speechless evening the day's last sun asked the final question: 'Who art thou?'

Again there was no reply.

27 July, 1941
Pratham diner surya prashna korechilo . . .
from 'Sesh Lekha'